Presented To:

_____

From:

_____

Date:

_____

Finding Reality
in Conflict, Confusion,
and Contradiction

STEVE C. SHANK

DESTINY IMAGE® PUBLISHERS, INC.

P.O. Box 310, Shippensburg, PA 17257-0310

"Promoting Inspired Lives."

This book and all other Destiny Image, Revival Press, MercyPlace, Fresh Bread, Destiny Image Fiction, and Treasure House books are available at Christian bookstores and distributors worldwide.

For a U.S. bookstore nearest you, call 1-800-722-6774.

For more information on foreign distributors, call 717-532-3040.

Reach us on the Internet: www.destinyimage.com.

ISBN 13 TP: 978-0-7684-4082-9

ISBN 13 Ebook: 978-0-7684-8914-9

For Worldwide Distribution, Printed in the U.S.A.

1 2 3 4 5 6 7 8 / 16 15 14 13 12

DEDICATION

In memory of
ROBERT W. SHANK
April 4, 1930—March 14, 2008
A greater dad no one has ever had!
I love you, and I'll see you soon.

This book is dedicated to all my fellow runners in the race of life who have tripped, fallen, and even missed a few hurdles—keep running and never look back! God has secured the victory for us all (see 2 Cor. 2:14).

Also, to all of you who pastor small churches (about 90 percent of us in America), be encouraged! Always remember the five loaves and the two fish, as well as Gideon's 300. The Lord does much with little! To Him be the glory forever.

ACKNOWLEDGMENTS

To Chanler, my wife; you are my best friend, my beauty, and my forever love. Thank you for standing faithfully with me through thick and thin. Your reward shall be great.

To my two daughters, Micah and Haven; you have always chosen the paths of righteousness and recognized the ways of wisdom. You are both great blessings to me.

To Mom and Dad; you have lived your lives unto God in all sincerity, without hypocrisy, and have impacted me and my children and grandchildren. I am forever grateful.

To my secretary of 29 years, Linda Holbrook; you've typed a lot of sermon notes for me and always kept the best of attitudes. I love and appreciate you, Linda.

To Martha Robbins; thank you so much for your help and advice with the manuscript of this book. You are one of the nicest people I know. May you have an eternal share in the rewards of this book.

ENDORSEMENTS

Steve C. Shank's book, *Schizophrenic God? Finding Reality in Conflict, Confusion, and Contradiction,* is a must-read for any sincere believer. It is the best book I have ever read dealing with the subject of God's sovereignty. Steve's thorough use of Scriptures, quotes from early church leaders, and real events happening today make this book come alive.

God has been blamed for way too much over the years, for things He never did. *"Every **good gift and every perfect gift is from above,** and comes down from the Father of lights, with whom there is no variableness, neither shadow of turning"* (James 1:17). This book will give you tremendous insight so you can properly discern what is from God, what is not, and how to stand firm in troubled times. A greatly needed book for the Body of Christ!

MARK R. ANDERSON

Evangelist and author of *Humility: The Hidden Key to Walking in Signs and Wonders*

www.markandersonministries.com

Schizophrenic God? is a wake-up call! Steve C. Shank has provided serious students of the Bible an antidote to a sleepy, passive, and complacent Church. His book gives a clear delineation of human responsibility in the face of demonic oppression and the need for active obedience to God along with forceful and intelligent resistance to satan so that God's Kingdom can be established on the earth.

JOAN HUNTER
Evangelist and author of *Endtime Economics*
www.joanhunter.org

When we first saw the manuscript of *Schizophrenic God?*, by our friend and fellow minister Steve C. Shank, we thought how difficult this must have been to write. This is an all-encompassing subject that has been debated and searched out since the dawn of human history. Since this topic has so many subjects and possibilities to cover, it would take nothing less than a knowledgeable author, dedicated scholar, and most importantly, a man of experience to precisely present this great discussion. Steve C. Shank is all of those things. He is a man acquainted with the world and no stranger in witnessing the human condition as it truly exists. His travels have given him unique opportunities to see the cry of humanity's heart and an intimate understanding of suffering. Through his knowledge of biblical studies, Steve is able to methodically dissect even the most difficult subjects contained in *Schizophrenic God?* and present a clear scriptural answer.

The wisdom contained in this book is for anyone who has sought answers to life's toughest questions. You will discover truths in Scripture that will give understanding to the questions you might have thought impossible to answer, and in doing so, you will have a clearer understanding of the unchanging heart of God.

TIM SCOTT and WILL DECKER
Missionaries, *Travel the Road* television series
www.traveltheroad.com

Along this journey called life, we are often hit hard and spun around by the winds of adversity. In these times, questions often arise that challenge our faith in the goodness of God. Steve C. Shank has presented in-depth evidence that when hardships, difficulties, and suffering invade our lives, it only comes from one source...the evil one. And just as convincingly, Steve has proven that the only Being in existence who is perfectly good is God. Not only is God good, but He is trustworthy, His Word is true, and we should always expect perfect goodness from Him. *"O taste and see that the Lord is good: blessed is the man that trusteth in Him"* (Ps. 34:8).

DR. SANDRA KENNEDY
Founder and Senior Pastor
Whole Life Ministries, Inc.
www.wholelife.org

This book presents answers to tough questions many ask today about the character of God. Steve C. Shank brilliantly deals with this task. He does not give us religious doctrines or rules that many people follow and find never work—religion disappoints and never changes people's lives. Steve paints a clear picture of the character of God as he discusses these important questions. The focus of this book is God and His goodness. After you finish reading this book, I believe your desire and hunger to know God and have fellowship with Him will be greatly stirred. Isn't this what really matters?

BISHOP NATALIA SCHEDRIVAYA
Evangelist and Founder
Village Gospel Harvest
Moscow, Russia
www.villagegospelharvest.ru

CONTENTS

INTRODUCTION

"Why?" "What happened?" "How did that occur?" We've all had mishaps, tragedies, and things happen in our lives that were hard to handle and even harder to explain, which caused us to ask such questions. When all the smoke had cleared, we said down deep in our hearts, "That just shouldn't have happened!"

But we continue to ask, "Was it simply meant to be? Was it Karma? Bad luck? The end result of a series of bad decisions? Are there unseen forces working against me? Was it the decision of a sovereign Judge somewhere out there in the universe?" We wonder, could the situation have been avoided? Will I face it again? Is there help? A way out? Can I recover after this tragedy bomb has exploded? Is there anything that can be solidly trusted?

After dealing and wrestling with questions like these over the past 30 years, I've discovered some answers. As we start this journey, I only ask one thing of you—to be willing to take off the shoes of your own understanding. By that, I mean this: Lay aside your preconceived ideas, your presuppositions, about why things happen in life. I will probably share some concepts that rock your current opinions. All I ask is that you keep an open mind and stay with me to the end. We will tackle some hard issues together that will have to be thoroughly thought through. But I firmly believe that when we get to the end of the tunnel, you will have experienced much more light on this important subject of "Why?"

Are you ready? Let's go!

Part I

WHY?

Chapter 1

WHY ALL THIS MESS?

After taking about 70 trips overseas to Latin America, Europe, Russia, Asia, Africa, the Orient, and the island nations of the world, I can say with all certainty that something has gone terribly wrong on planet Earth! Deception, despair, destitution, disease, and death continually decimate the human race day after day. This is not theory I'm talking about or a subject to be debated in our institutions of higher learning. Why is all this heart-wrenching destruction happening? What or who is behind it all? Is there a way to deal with it?

We've heard all the hollow, pat answers that don't ring true and leave us still wondering:

- "You never know what God's going to do. Who can understand the ways of God?"

- "There's always a reason behind everything God does."

- "We'll understand it better in the sweet by and by."

- "The Lord's ways are mysterious and past finding out."

- "God is testing you, and if it doesn't kill you, you'll come through it stronger."

- "God is punishing you. You need to learn a lesson from this."

- "This is God's way of teaching you to deepen your spirituality."

Instead of learning through tragedy, many people come away bitter and distraught. Disillusioned, they ask, "Is this the kind of God I'm supposed to love and trust?" We've all seen things happen in life that ended in wretched, miserable outcomes adversely affecting all who were connected to the situation. We've been taught generation after generation that "God's got it all under control, and this somehow works toward a higher good." Are you ready to put this teaching under the microscope?

Passive acceptance of everything being the will of a higher power was practiced by the ancient Stoics and is practiced by many Middle Eastern religions today. For instance, Islam teaches that Allah decides your destiny before birth, prepares everything that happens to you, what kind of life you'll have, etc.

The Koran teaches that everything that happens to you is the will of Allah and has been decided by him before you experience it: "Nothing occurs, either in the earth or in yourselves, without its being in a Book before we make it happen.

That is something easy for Allah."[1] "Allah created both you and what you do."[2] According to these verses, every moment in the life of every person has been predetermined by Allah. Every event that has been arranged by him is what is best and most appropriate for us. Nothing can happen that has not been created by him and willed by him. Allah has determined everyone's fate.

That line of religious thought is very similar to the belief system held by many Christians today. But interestingly enough, this concept did not begin to be propagated in the Christian church until the time of the early church father, Augustine. Augustine taught that "nothing happens unless the Omnipotent wills it to happen."[3] He also taught that a suffering victim "ought not to attribute [his suffering] to the will of men, or of angels, or of any created spirit, but rather to His [God's] will."[4] From this line of logic, Augustine encouraged victimized Christians to find peace and security in the knowledge that their oppressors could not have harmed them unless God allowed it for a greater good. Augustine lived around A.D. 400, and, without question, we can see how his teaching caught on and was passed down from generation to generation. In the 1500s, John Calvin taught that "all events are governed by God's secret plan."[5]

Now, dear reader, don't bail out on me. Let's sum this up and think it through together. What's been taught for generations is this: God ordains or causes all things that happen in life, or He simply allows them to occur; and, behind every event, God has a specific purpose. Let's put this common belief under the microscope.

WARNING! PROCEED WITH CAUTION!

I am now going to cite some true stories. Remember, these are real people who loved and were loved by their families. Try to imagine someone you have known and loved experiencing these atrocities. Let's get ready to grapple with these tough issues of life that are hitting people right now around the globe. May we no longer be satisfied with impractical, "ivory tower" answers to these most serious problems in life. (Note: These true stores get increasingly worse, so you may want to read the first one and skip over the rest.)

Our first case happened in 1983 in a typical middle-class neighborhood in the suburbs of Denver, Colorado. A little three-year-old, blonde-haired, blue-eyed girl was sitting out in front of her house eating a Popsicle. Her dad stepped inside, and in an instant, she was gone. Three long days went by with no trace of her. Then as two people were hiking in the foothills, they heard a shrill, high-pitched sound. What was that? They followed the sound and then clearly heard, "Mommy!"

"Where are you?" they called out.

The small voice called back, "I'm here!"

To their utter dismay, they found her 12 feet down in the bottom of an outhouse. "What are you doing there?" they asked the little voice.

"I live here," was her faint reply.

She was wearing only her panties and had survived three terrifying nights in the frigid filth of that outhouse. Her abductor had done the unimaginable to her and then dumped her like defecated matter into a pit of human waste.

The Bible says that God is love (see 1 John 4:8). What kind of being would plan such a thing for an object of his love? Had God willed this to happen to this helpless little three-year-old? If so, for what purpose?

The next two reports were taken from the book, *I Was Saddam's Son*.[6] They involved Saddam Hussein's eldest son, Uday. They are not for the faint of heart.

One day after returning from duck hunting, Uday Hussein spotted a young couple walking in the garden near the al Medina Hotel. They were on their honeymoon, having been married the day before. Uday found the woman attractive and wanted her at any cost. He grabbed her by the arm and said, "You're much too good for this simple person. Come with me to my suite." It mattered not that her husband was a captain, in uniform, and had faithfully served Iraq for ten years. This man screamed at Uday and tried to defend his young bride. He was subsequently retained and beaten brutally by the ever-present bodyguards.

The new bride was brought to Uday's suite, where she steadfastly refused all of his advances. He finally flew into a rage, beat her until she could no longer defend herself, and then violated her. After he had left the room, a long, piercing scream was heard. She had jumped off the balcony from the seventh floor to an instant death. Her husband was sent to a prison called "The Palace Where It Ends," where he was executed by a firing squad. His crime? "Insulting the President."[7]

Now I ask you, do you believe all things are of God? Governed by His secret plan? Can you envision yourself officiating at this funeral and telling the grieving parents that this was God's divine blueprint for these newlyweds?

Here's our last case: According to the official report, Nahle Sabet, a pretty young student of architecture, had "simply disappeared." In reality, she had been abducted and taken to the farm of Uday Hussein. She refused to respond to his sexual advances, so she was repeatedly raped, beaten, and abused until Uday lost interest in her. Then he locked her in the kennels with his famished attack dogs—Rottweilers, Great Danes, and Dobermans.[8]

Why? Who or what is behind such unspeakable crimes and injustices? Pat answers like "God's got it all under control" don't cut it. In fact, those answers border on being thoughtless, heartless, and even ridiculous!

What about diseases like the 1918 influenza outbreak? It killed 30 million people worldwide, including 550,000 Americans. In comparison, the U.S. lost over 400,000 to military deaths in World War II. If victimized by the 1918 flu, a person could go to bed well and by morning be dead. Once the flu took effect, people's lungs began to fill with fluid and they had trouble breathing; their temperature would shoot through the roof, their skin turned black and blue, and their hair began to fall out. Was this a punishment of God?

Why all the mess-ups, catastrophes, and downright cruel, heart-wrenching events that continue on a daily basis? Surely a God who is paying attention could not idly stand by and allow all these daily disasters to happen.

If God's running everything in the universe, and He's got everything under control, are we sure He's a full-grown

Supreme Sovereign, or is He a spiritual adolescent-type of being who thinks He'll never be accountable for His actions?

Is God the original schizophrenic?

Well, no, He isn't, and there are some real answers to all of these "Whys"! Are you ready to move forward? Let's go!

Chapter 2

WHY ALL THIS CONFUSION?

Was the world designed to be so chaotic, confusing, and downright dangerous—or was it made for everything to function in a harmonious, orderly way? Was it originally intended to be a loving and safe environment for all who dwell here?

Some people tell me, "I have a dysfunctional family," and I tell them, "You have a dysfunctional world!"

Let's look at two predominant views. But before we do, let's look at the definition of a few terms.

Most people believe that God is *sovereign;* and of course, if God is God, He *is* sovereign. The dictionary defines *sovereign* as "having supreme rank, power, or authority."[1] In other words, He's at the top of the ladder. There is no one above Him. God is also *omnipotent,* which means He's all-powerful, possessing unlimited power. He's also *omnipresent,* which simply means He's always present everywhere.

THE EXTREME SOVEREIGNTY VIEW

With those things in mind, let's examine the first world-view, which I call the "extreme sovereignty" view. As we closely look at this view, I will explain why I call it *extreme*. Most people, whether atheists or firm believers, may be shocked to discover that they have parts of this view imbedded in their belief systems.

The extreme sovereignty view reasons that since God is sovereign, omnipotent, and omnipresent, He also exercises *omnicontrol*. In other words, God has predestined and pre-ordered everything that happens in life; whatever happens, God either causes it or allows it as part of His divine plan and will. An event wouldn't have happened unless God willed it because God exercises omnicontrol. This view says all things are prearranged in the plan of God, and there's a divine reason behind everything that happens in life.

According to this view, God decides the destiny of all human beings and orchestrates all that happens in the world, even the evil. Whatever happens to you in life—period—is God's sovereign will. The ultimate reason behind *why* everything happens is God. God is the ultimate *why*. Things that look "evil" somehow fit into God's overall plan for good; God must have some wise, loving purpose behind them.

This view reasons that if God is good and controls all things, then all things must be good or loving or just. We are to accept them as coming from the loving hand of a God who in His sovereignty has some kind of divine purpose behind it. So when cancers, car wrecks, or divorces occur, people who believe this view give pat answers such as: "There's a purpose for everything. God has His reasons." "His ways are mysterious and past finding out." "All is still under His control, and remember that God is sovereign."

The word *sovereign* is not used in the King James Version of the Bible, and when the concept is used, it is never used in the manner in which the extreme sovereignty view defines it. This view leaves people with a passive, *"Que sera, sera;* whatever will be, will be"* attitude about life. This view in its extreme form tells us that all things are of God, so God is behind all things. However, if you see God behind all things, you then see God behind all evil. In effect, you are calling good evil; worse yet, you are calling God evil!

Is it any wonder that so many people are terrified of God and inwardly feel that He has a dark, malicious side to His nature? How can we ever know what God's going to do? This view leaves us in doubt about the nature of God and the will of God because it paints the picture of good and evil coming to us from the hand of the same God. This view leaves people with a big sigh of resignation, and all they can say is, "Well, God is sovereign."

Go with me now on my first trip overseas. I had never been out of the United States, not even to Mexico or Canada. You can imagine the shock that hit me when I arrived in Bombay, India. About ten million people are homeless and sleep every night on the streets of this massive city. I was completely stunned, and I wept for two days over the scenes that confronted me. Crushing poverty and debilitating diseases made me keenly aware that the earth is filled with horrifying suffering and diabolical evil.

In India, I came face to face with a man whose nose and lips had been eaten off by leprosy. His appearance had taken on the form of part man, part skeleton! I knew from the depths of my soul that it was never God's intention for the love of His heart, the human race, to be trapped in this type of horror-movie existence. This was not the will of an all-loving God.

THE JESUS WORLDVIEW

With that as a background, let's explore the second worldview, which I will call "the Jesus worldview." The historical character, Jesus of Nazareth, was actually God becoming a human being or *"the Word was made flesh"* (John 1:14). He was the full revelation or explanation of God (see John 1:18), actually showing us what God is like. He even told one of His followers, *"He who has seen Me has seen the Father* [God]" (John 14:9 NKJV).

I challenge you to approach Jesus and His worldview as if this is your first time to ever hear about Him. Lay aside all your preconceived notions and notice the character, heart, actions, and will of Jesus of Nazareth as He is so carefully portrayed in the Bible in the Books of Matthew, Mark, Luke, and John.

Jesus burst upon the scene when He began His ministry. He approached life as if He was entering a war zone! He came to the rescue of a victimized, suffering human race. Every person He touched, He treated with mercy and compassion. He treated them as if they were casualties of war. Now remember that Jesus is *"the exact representation"* of God's nature (Heb. 1:3 NASB). Jesus is "re-presenting" God to the human race. Everything about Jesus *represents* God exactly (see Heb. 1:3).

Therefore, Jesus is the great Revealer of God to you. He reveals God's heart, God's attitude, and God's desire toward life and the human race. Watch how Jesus approached the brokenhearted, the sick, the suffering, the confused, the guilt-ridden, and the downtrodden, and there you will see the will of God in action. Jesus is the will of God in an earth suit; and when He entered the war zone on planet Earth, He aggressively challenged the disasters and dilemmas of humanity.

Just a little side note here—in my travels around the world, I have noticed that the majority of the people of the world believe that there is a real, invisible spiritual realm that is inhabited by spirit beings. From this spirit realm, things can be determined and set into motion in the physical realm. These parts of the world (India, Asia, Africa, South America) see a steady stream of miraculous occurrences taking place; things happen that cannot be explained by human logic.

In contrast, countries in the West (U.S., Canada, Britain, France, Spain, etc.) believe that the world is all physical and material. This puts us out of step with the vast majority of people groups of the world; and, consequently, we see and experience less of the miraculous.

Is there a realm of spirits, a spiritual realm, or is there not? How would we ever know?

I appeal to Jesus! Throughout this journey you will hear me make that statement. Jesus said that He was "the Truth," or that reality was found in Him (see John 14:6). In a judicial system, there is always a final court of appeal. Jesus' life and words are the supreme court of appeal—the final authority—where all issues about life can be settled.

Here's where the confusion has entered in: people have allowed their logic, opinions, and experiences in life to determine truth for them instead of settling the issue that Jesus knows the truth and tells the truth, and that reality can only be found in Him. If my opinion about matters in life contradicts or doesn't agree with Jesus' words or actions, guess whose opinion is invalid? Mine! I don't have the wisdom, experience, or audacity to say, "Oh, no, Jesus! I'm right, and You're all wrong!"

Let's recap these two contrasting views:

Extreme sovereignty worldview—God has predestined or preordered everything that happens in life. God exercises omnicontrol, so you have no choice or will in the matter. If something happens, God willed it for you. If something fails to happen, it was not His will. Whatever happens in life, God either causes it or allows it as part of His divine will and plan. In this blueprint plan, it is believed that even evil things that happen will somehow bring about good in the end. God's will is the ultimate reason behind every event in life.

Jesus' worldview—Jesus approached the world as if something had terribly gone wrong, "An enemy has done this!" (see Matt. 13:28). Jesus does not view everything that has happened as the will of God, but with determination He resolves to reverse the curse of suffering and heartache that has blasted the human race. Jesus brought healing, deliverance, and relief to people, treating them as if they were casualties of war. Jesus' worldview does not show us that everything that happens in life is always God's will; He actually waged war on that which was *not* God's will by helping the unfortunate out of their predicaments. Jesus' life and world-view clearly show us that there are wills, other than God's will, at work on planet Earth.

As you will see in the next chapter, these are two very differing and opposing views!

Chapter 3

PASSIVELY ACCEPT OR AGGRESSIVELY RESIST?

I heard a man say recently that his favorite statement about Jesus was found in First John 3:8 (NASB), *"The Son of God appeared for this purpose, to destroy the works of the devil."* That statement shines a lot of light on our subject! It shows us that there are works on earth that are *not* the works of God; and, since Jesus came to destroy these works, they are clearly not the will of God. Whatever Jesus opposed and destroyed are works of the devil and not of God! Before we study this issue closely, however, we need to answer this question: Who is this one called "the devil"?

First of all, he is not some comic book character with horns, tail, and a red suit. When the Bible refers to the devil, it is not referring to just a symbol of all that epitomizes evil. No, this is a real, personal, spirit being from whom all evil proceeds and who has a whole host of lesser-ranking spirit beings who help him carry out his bad intentions.

The devil is a "created spirit" who exercises a will that does not align or agree with the will of God. The Bible compares the devil to a devouring lion (see 1 Pet. 5:8), a wolf (see John 10:12), a serpent (see Rev. 12:9), a trap-setter (see Ps. 91:3), an enemy (see Matt. 13:28), and a thief (see John 10:10). Lions rip and tear, wolves eat sheep, serpents are sneaky and strike with poison, traps put us in bondage, enemies try to defeat us, and thieves take away what is rightfully ours.

So the reason Jesus came was to destroy the works of these enemies of ours. You might be thinking that you don't believe in demonic beings? Well, Jesus did; so I appeal to Jesus as final authority!

Notice the contrast here: Jesus said, *"My purpose is to give life in all its fullness."* (John 10:10 NLT). The human race was void of this kind of life. Jesus had just said, *"The thief's purpose is to steal and kill and destroy"* (John 10:10 NLT). Jesus' purpose and the purpose of the devil are clearly contrasted here. Jesus called the devil *"a murderer from the beginning"* and *"the father of lies,"* whose purpose is to keep people from the truth (John 8:44 NLT).

Jesus' worldview in capsulated form is beautifully stated here: *"He went about doing good and healing all who were oppressed by the devil, for God was with Him"* (Acts 10:38 NASB). We clearly see that what Jesus did was God's will; that it was God's will to heal all who Jesus came in contact with; that Jesus only brought good into people's lives; and that all who needed healing were oppressed by the devil.

The world that Jesus came into was clearly seen to be in bondage to the evil one! Jesus came to wage war on the devil, to set his captives free, and to give humanity true life in all its fullness. To see what this looks like, *let's follow Jesus* in His earth walk, paying close attention to His worldview and His life practices.

One day as Jesus was teaching, He met a woman who was bent over double and had been in this condition for 18 years. Jesus said, *"Satan has kept her bound for eighteen years. Isn't it right to set her free...?"* (Luke 13:16 CEV[1]). What was Jesus doing? Destroying the works of the devil and healing all who were oppressed by him. Notice that satan had kept her bound, but Jesus set her free. There was no confusion over whether God wanted her to be healed or not.

Let's look at another case that also reveals Jesus' worldview: A man had brought his young son to Jesus' disciples for help. The son was mute and was regularly overcome by severe seizures. The disciples had tried their best and were unable to bring any relief or freedom to the son. Many Christians today would have said at this point, "Maybe God has some unknown sovereign purpose, and that's why He's not helped and released this boy." When Jesus comes on the scene, however, He never gives this response, "Did you ever consider that it might be God's sovereign will to keep him bound?"

The father knew that a demonic spirit was the source of the problem. He told Jesus, *"Often he* [the demonic spirit] *has thrown him both into the fire and into the water to destroy him"* (Mark 9:22 NKJV). It was clear to the father that an enemy was trying to "destroy" his son. He knew this was not the sovereign will of God, and he did not embrace it as such.

Notice how Jesus viewed this situation. *"...He rebuked the unclean spirit, saying to it, 'You deaf and mute spirit, I command*

you, come out of him and do not enter him again'" (Mark 9:25
NASB). Jesus was simply doing God's will and healing all
who were oppressed by the devil.

Just as evil adults victimize children against God's will,
rapists victimize women against God's will, and heartless
dictators victimize their subjects against God's will, you can
see that these demonic invaders can victimize others against
God's will.

Jesus never hinted that these evil spirits were carrying out
an all-wise, sovereign plan of God. He treated these people
as victims of enemy invaders and as captives who needed to
be set free! Jesus devoted His ministry to removing spiritual
parasites from their victims by healing and deliverance. He
never can be seen searching for a divine, hidden will behind
evil. Not once does Jesus ask questions like, "What is God's
sovereign purpose in this?" "Why would God allow this?"
"How could God do this?" Too many people today are asking
questions that Jesus never asked because they're not accepting the revelation that He brought!

As you carefully study Jesus' worldview, it becomes
increasingly clear that He always took a stand against anything that purposed to "steal, kill, and destroy."

For example, a situation is recorded in Mark 4:35-39 in
which Jesus and His disciples enter a boat at night to travel
across the sea. In the middle of the night, a storm of hurri-
cane proportions arises and threatens to kill Jesus and His
disciples. How does Jesus view this situation? *"He arose and
rebuked the wind, and said to the sea, 'Peace, be still!'"* (Mark
4:39 NKJV). For us to make an honest assessment of this

situation, we have to say that the origin of this storm was not of God. Jesus "rebuked" the storm just as He did when casting demons out of people.

A rebuke is a command that releases God's power and authority in subduing His enemies. So when Jesus rebukes the storm, He is obviously speaking a word of authority against the enemy in order to subdue him. The source of this storm was demonic, and Jesus treated it like a demon who was attempting to steal, kill, and destroy. This is another crystal-clear example of the Jesus worldview.

If you say this storm was ultimately from God, then you've got Jesus rebuking God, which results in a divided kingdom. Jesus said that a kingdom divided against itself cannot stand (see Matt. 12:25). If we make Jesus our final authority, who settles all issues about life and truth, we must conclude that "sovereignty" does not mean that God is behind and in control of all things.

Let me ask you a question: When evil comes against you and has the potential to steal, kill, or destroy, which do you cry out: "Why, God?" or "I rebuke you, devil!" If you answered with the second response, you're in sync with the Jesus worldview.

I realize that most people respond with, "Why, God?" This is a clear indicator that shows they believe that God is behind and in control of all things. Even our insurance policies define *acts of God* as, "a manifestation especially of a violent or destructive natural force, such as lightning strike or earthquake."[2]

As I stated earlier, the belief that God is behind all things seems to have started with the church father Augustine about A.D. 400. He taught that "nothing happens unless the Omnipotent wills it to happen."[3] He taught that a suffering victim "ought not to attribute [suffering] to the will of men, or of angels, or of any created spirit, but rather to His [God's] will."[4] That does not agree with Jesus' worldview because we are clearly told that those He helped and healed were "*oppressed of the devil*" (Acts 10:38).

Augustine's "extreme sovereignty" theory took root and became a widespread belief. As previously mentioned, John Calvin taught in the 1500s that, "all events are governed by God's secret plan."[5] So it's understandable that even modern-day dictionaries and insurance policies define natural disasters as *acts of God*. But did the early church fathers share this extreme "sovereignty" worldview?

EARLY CHURCH FATHERS

As we look at the worldview of some of these early church fathers, keep in mind that they lived approximately 250 years before Augustine. Although the earliest church fathers did not hold to the extreme sovereignty view, you will see that they already had to begin refuting such views as early as A.D. 100.

Justin Martyr, A.D. 100-165: "But the angels transgressed this appointment.... They afterward subdued the human race to themselves...and among men they sowed murders, wars, adulteries, intemperate deeds, *and all wickedness*."[6] Notice, however, from Justin's next statement that even back then, about 100 years after Jesus' earth walk, people began to place the blame for all evil upon God, "Where also the poets and mythologists, not knowing that it was the angels and those demons who...did these things...ascribed them to God Himself."[7]

Clement of Alexandria, A.D. 150-215, said, "So in no respect is God the author of evil...since free choice and inclination originate sins."[8]

According to the early church fathers, the tragic and terrible current state of the world is caused by angels and humans misusing their free wills. Jesus instructed us to pray that God's will would be done on earth as it is in Heaven (see Matt. 6:10). Why would there be a need to pray that if everything that happens on earth was already God's will? This presupposes that God's will is *not* always being done on earth.

Tertullian, A.D. 160-220: "Diseases and other grievous calamities are the result of demons whose great business is the ruin of mankind."[9] He further clearly stated, "It is not the part of good and solid faith to refer all things to the will of God."[10] As you can see, this fits the Jesus worldview of First John 3:8 (NASB), *"The Son of God appeared for this purpose, to destroy the works of the devil."*

Origen, A.D. 185-254, believed that "evils do not proceed from God.... Famine, blasting of the vine and fruit trees, pestilence among men and beasts: all these are the proper occupations of demons." So, too, demons are "the cause of plagues...barrenness...tempests...and similar calamities."[11] The common belief today is that these are all *acts of*

God. You can clearly see from these and the preceding statements that the early church did not hold to that belief.

Augustine's later doctrines of predestination, all things being the will of God, and his theory of evil always being part of God's mysterious plan for people, is a radical departure from Jesus' worldview and that of the earlier church fathers.

It's interesting to note that as you read books and articles from the extreme sovereignty viewpoint, you find very little mention of the devil or demons; satan is conspicuously missing! Why would there need to be any emphasis upon the evil one if you believed that all things are of God and He's predestined and prearranged everything that happens in life? Extreme sovereignty teaches you to embrace or at least passively accept all events that come your way because they are all part of the sovereign will of God and ultimately serve God's secret plan for your life. As Calvin so clearly explained this viewpoint, "All events are governed by God's secret plan."[12]

If we passively accept the thought that God's will is behind every evil intent and event in life, we mistakenly end up accepting things that are coming at us from satan as coming from a loving Father God! In doing so, we terribly tarnish the nature of God. We defame His character and open the door for false accusations to be brought against the One who Jesus said is the only One who is perfectly good! (See Mark 10:18.)

In contrast to this view that teaches "all comes from God, therefore we must embrace it," the Bible actually teaches, *"Resist the devil, and he will flee from you"* (James 4:7). The

Greek word used for resist is loaded with military connotations. As you can see in this rendering, *"Make war on the Evil One and he will be put to flight before you"* (James 4:7 BEV).

If the devil is one of the tools under God's control whose purpose is to work God's will into your life, why would God tell you to resist him? This makes it clear that we are to receive what is *of* God and resist what is *not!* What satan brings against you does not sovereignly equal God's will for your life. Satan does not love you and have a wonderful plan for your life; neither is he a co-laborer together with God.

In Ephesians 6:13, we are told that there are times when we can come under an enemy attack from hostile spirits. In order to come through these attacks victoriously, we must be clothed in the full armor of God and aggressively resist the attempts of these spiritual terrorists to bring us down in the midst of these occasions that the Bible calls "the evil day." Notice how we are clearly shown again that evil must be resisted for the good will of God to prevail in our lives:

> *Use every piece of God's armor to resist the enemy in the time of evil, so that after the battle you will still be standing firm* (Ephesians 6:13 NLT).

So we can clearly see that there are times that an evil one, an enemy, tries to impose his evil will upon us. We are told to resist this evil one and stand against his evil will in those evil days of attack—no passive acceptance of everything in life being the predetermined will of a sovereign God! We can clearly see that the Bible, Jesus, and the early church teach that there is an evil will behind all evil deeds; as Origen said,

"Evils do not proceed from God."[13] God is adamantly against all the works of the devil—every murder, theft, lie, rape, act of unfaithfulness—God is *against* all of that. Everything that is loving, true, kind, merciful, and full of compassion, He is *for* all of that.

So many in the United States today are passively accepting everything that happens in life as the sovereign will of God. By accepting this extreme sovereignty worldview, the root of complacency has sunk deep into the heart of the American church. Jesus' ministry was never one of resignation, but one of revolt against satan and his works of destruction. Jesus' life and ministry never taught us to see God behind all of life's circumstances, but to stand against an enemy invader who seeks to steal, kill, destroy, and oppress! He went forth as an aggressive Warrior and routed demonic forces, bringing the good will of God into people's lives. The Kingdom of God advances as captives are delivered and set free!

When Jesus came on the scene, He entered a war zone—planet Earth. His ministry was an all-out attack on the enemies of God and humanity. Jesus was always grieved and angered by the suffering and oppression inflicted upon God's children. How then can those oppressive works come from God's sovereignty? Jesus is our model, our example, our pattern Man. In His teachings and life practices—in His worldview—we find our perfect theology.

Let's wrap up this phase of our journey by saying that we live in the midst of a cosmic war, and in a state of war—bullets fly, bombs explode, mines are stepped on, prisoners are taken captive, people are raped, and all types of atrocities are committed. The earth is filled with horrifying suffering and diabolical evil. Hostile, evil forces are seeking to destroy the love of God's heart—that's us, the human race.

According to the Bible, Jesus, and the early church fathers, suffering and evil are not part of God's sovereign plan, but rather the result of angels and humans misusing their free will. We must now consider this question: Do we really have free will?

Chapter 4

FATE OR FREE WILL?

Presupposition, assumption, premise—we all have one—a starting point upon which our belief system is based and a conclusion drawn. What do you believe about God? About life and its experience? How do you interpret what's coming your way? Do you have the ability to make decisions that will determine your destiny, or has God decided and predestined everything that will ever happen to you in life?

FATE

Webster defines *fate* as "something that unavoidably befalls a person...the universal principle or ultimate agency by which the order of things is presumably prescribed...that which is inevitably predetermined."[1] To review, the extreme sovereignty view believes that "nothing happens unless the Omnipotent wills it to happen"[2]; that "all events are governed by God's secret plan"[3]; and that "nothing happens apart from divine determination and decree."[4]

Islam is the second largest religion in the world today, with an estimated 1.2 billion adherents. It also teaches that "nothing occurs, either in the earth or in yourselves, without its being in a Book before we make it happen.... Allah created both you and what you do."[5]

According to this viewpoint, God decides the destiny of all human beings. He orchestrates everything that happens in the world, even the evil. He's a God of omnicontrol; He preordains and predestines everything that happens. People go to Heaven, get healed, and are delivered from calamities solely by God's arbitrary, sovereign choice; or they go to hell, fail to get healed, or die a calamitous death because that is God's sovereign will for that individual. The ultimate reason behind *why* everything happens is God. God is the ultimate *why*.

If this presupposition is true, logic would tell you that free will is impossible. If God has preplanned all things and controls all things, then you can't have a free will. That's the exact conclusion at which millions of people have arrived.

Charles Spurgeon was one of the most influential preachers of the 1800s. He was called the "prince of preachers." It was estimated that his ministry touched about ten million people. Spurgeon stated, "Philosophy and religion both discard at once the very thought of free will. Free will is nonsense."[6] In an even stronger statement, Spurgeon said, "I believe that the free will heresy assails the sovereignty of God."[7]

Proponents of the extreme sovereignty viewpoint say that God controls everything that happens in the world, and if the individual can control any aspect of his or her life, that would be the same as telling God what to do. From that line of reasoning they conclude that God can't be God and remain sovereign if a person has free will or the ability to choose. According to this logic, they conclude that God has randomly chosen an "elect" few to go to Heaven. They argue, "If Jesus had died for the whole world, the whole world would be saved because God's will cannot be defeated or resisted. It's obvious that Jesus did not die for everyone because everyone does not get saved."

CHOICE

Webster defines *choice* as: "alternative, option, prefer-ence...the power of choosing between things. Choice implies the opportunity to choose...free right or privilege of choos-ing: to exercise one's option."[8] Has God, in His sovereignty, given all rational creatures a free will? Do people really have a God-given privilege to choose between things?

Early church father Origen (A.D. 185-254) believed that God rules in a way that is consistent with "the preservation of freedom of will in all rational creatures."[9] Early church father Irenaeus (A.D. 120-205) clearly stated that "in man, as well as in angels, [God] has placed the power of choice."[10] Athe-nagoras (A.D. 133-190) believed, "Just as with men, who have freedom of choice as to both virtue and vice, so it is among the angels."[11]

If it is true that we have free will, God has given each one of us an awesome privilege but has also placed upon us an awesome responsibility. We can choose to go God's way or we can choose to go our own way. We can choose God's gift of Heaven and eternal life or choose to reject His gracious offer. In fact, where every issue in life is concerned, we can shun the wrong and choose the right or vice versa. So it's clear from this viewpoint that just because God wills something for an individual doesn't mean His will automatically comes to pass. If the individual chooses a way or a will other than God's, then what God planned for him or her does not necessarily come to pass.

In order to settle these most important questions about life, we're going to have to go to the Final Court of Appeal—the Eternal Scriptures. But before we do, I need to challenge you with some important observations.

I was recently told about a survey that reported some surprising conclusions. The report stated that when most people are presented with irrefutable facts that prove their own presuppositions and opinions are wrong, the majority will still choose to believe their own false opinions! In other words, they will choose to go with the wrong rather than the right and continue to live believing in lies rather than the truth.

This confirms what I've heard a friend of mine say repeatedly. He says most Christians won't let the Bible get in the way of what they already believe. If you're in that category, this is a great time to get out of it!

Let's start with Jesus—the Personification of all truth. Notice this in Matthew 23:37 (NASB):

> *Jerusalem, Jerusalem, who kills the prophets and stones those who are sent to her! How often I wanted to gather your children together, the way a hen gathers her chicks under her wings, and you were unwilling.*

My Bible has a heading over this portion of Scripture entitled, "Lament over Jerusalem." Jesus is expressing real grief and sorrow over the fact that what He willed for Jerusalem could not take place because the inhabitants were unwilling. If God in His sovereignty had already determined this outcome, wouldn't Jesus have known it? Better yet, if Jesus knew that His Father was behind this, why the grief and sorrow?

Moses exhorted the people in Deuteronomy 30:19 (NASB):

> *I call heaven and earth to witness against you today, that I have set before you life and death, the blessing and the curse. So choose life in order that you may live, you and your descendants.*

Why would these people be told to choose if God had already predestined whether their lives would be blessed or cursed? This Scripture makes it very clear that God wanted His blessing and life to be upon all of them, but they had to exercise their free will and power of choice.

Then there's Joshua's classic statement that you see hanging on many doors throughout the world:

> *If it is disagreeable in your sight to serve the Lord, choose for yourselves today whom you will serve… but as for me and my house, we will serve the Lord"* (Joshua 24:15 NASB).

Joshua clearly tells the people that the "choice" is theirs and that they should choose *today*. He also shows his belief in a free will when he says, *We will serve the Lord.*

Isaiah shows us that everything we do is not always what God has planned for us. *'Woe to the rebellious children,'* declares the Lord, *'who execute a plan, but not Mine, and make an alliance, but not of My Spirit...'* (Isa. 30:1 NASB).

It becomes clear as you read through the entire Bible that God's purpose for our lives doesn't automatically come to pass; we can choose to accept it or reject it. *"But the Pharisees and the lawyers rejected God's purpose for themselves, not having been baptized by John"* (Luke 7:30 NASB). This Scripture clearly shows us that God's purpose can be *rejected*. God, in His sovereignty, has chosen to give humanity a free will. Your choice determines your own eternal destiny!

HEAVEN OR HELL—GOD'S CHOICE OR YOUR CHOICE?

We've already seen that the extreme sovereignty viewpoint starts out with the premise that God has already predetermined everything that happens in every individual's life. This of course includes your eternal destiny. This belief states that God has "predestined" a small group of people called the "elect" to escape hell and live eternally in Heaven. The majority of people will spend eternity in hell because that's what God has chosen for them (before they were even born).

If you are fortunate enough to find yourself in the group called the "elect," it's simply because God has arbitrarily chosen you. You are one of God's random choices! I would compare you to a lottery winner. But does God make all your choices for you or do you have the God-given power to choose for yourself? Did Jesus die for the whole world or just for an elect few? Let's go to the Eternal Scriptures.

> *And He [that same Jesus Himself] is the propitiation (the atoning sacrifice) for our sins, and not for ours alone but also for [the sins of] the whole world* (1 John 2:2 AMP).

His saving grace was not just provided for an elect few, but for the whole world. *"Who is ever willing for all mankind to be saved and to come to an increasing knowledge of the truth"* (1 Tim. 2:4 Williams[12]). Once again we see that God is willing for all humankind to be saved.

Again we see this in Titus 2:11 (Williams): *"For God's favor has appeared with its offer of salvation to all mankind."* Sad to say, there are many who are choosing to reject God's gracious offer of salvation, just as the Pharisees rejected God's purpose for themselves back in Jesus' time.

Thank God that this Scripture holds true for all humanity: *"He is really dealing patiently with you, because He is not willing for any to perish but for all to have an opportunity to repent"* (2 Peter 3:9b Williams). What a great privilege to be able to choose God's way, His gracious offer of salvation through Jesus Christ! Your choice also carries with it a great responsibility because your choice determines your destiny.

DIVINE PUPPETEER IN THE SKY?

If everything that happens in life is preplanned by God, and no one has freedom of will or the power to choose, we must conclude that God is simply a master puppeteer. Would a world full of puppets be worth creating? How much pleasure could He derive from forced worship?

If God is in complete control of all humans and every event and circumstance in life, how does that differ from pro wrestling? All the wrestlers are simply following a script that's already been planned out for them. The whole thing is staged, and the outcome has already been determined for each one of them. Do you really believe that because God is "sovereign" that means He controls all actions and all events, and that He's predetermined all things?

In the story Jesus told about the prodigal son in Luke 15, why would the father get so happy and throw a party to celebrate his son's return? (See Luke 15:32.) Didn't the father share the extreme sovereignty view that says the lost son was preprogrammed to come back? How could the prodigal, lost son say, "*I will arise and go to my father*" (Luke 15:18) if he didn't have the power to choose or freedom of will?

We're also told in Luke 15:10 (NASB) that "*there is joy in the presence of the angels of God over one sinner who repents.*" If the sinner was preprogrammed to repent and all the angels are preprogrammed to rejoice, what exactly is the point of all this?

The testimony of Job would have no meaning or virtue at all if God had already preprogrammed Job's choice to remain faithful. After Job had lost all that he had and was devastated, "*Then his wife said to him, 'Do you still hold fast your integrity? Curse God and die!'*" (Job 2:9 NASB). Was there a chance that Job could have renounced God, or had God sovereignly chosen for Job to remain faithful?

If you choose the latter answer, then you must say that everything that happens in life is God's sovereign will, everything you do in life is what God has already chosen for you to do, and you are simply a robotic actor carrying out your role in God's great cosmic theater of life.

A DETERMINED TIME TO DIE?

Most people that I know, whether Christian or non-Christian, believe that each person has a "set" time to die. We would have to put that under the category of fate ("that which is inevitably predetermined"). So if people believe they have a "set" time to die, they actually have some aspect of the extreme sovereignty viewpoint in their belief system. Where did that come from?

Many Christians will say that Hebrews 9:27 teaches that there is an appointed time for each of us to die, when in actuality it says, *"It is appointed for men to die once and after this comes judgment"* (Heb. 9:27 NASB). This clearly shows us that every person will die—death is unavoidable. It shows us that there are no do-overs, no second chances, no reincarnations. It shows us that after our inevitable death comes an appointment with judgment when we will each give an account for our life. What it does not say is that God has set a predetermined time for us to die.

People might object and say that Ecclesiastes 3:2 teaches that God has set a time for each individual's death. Ecclesiastes 3:2 states that there is, *"A time to be born, and a time to die."* All human beings have a birth date and time; likewise, every human being will have a death date and time. If you're a human being, your birth and your death are unavoidable facts of life.

Now here's the issue we want to look at through the eyes of the Eternal Word of God. Can you, by your own choice, shorten or prolong your lifespan on the earth, or do you have no choice about this or any other matter, with the day and manner of your death having already been predetermined by God?

Ephesians 6:1-3 (NASB) states, *"Children, obey your parents in the Lord, for this is right. Honor your father and mother (which is the first commandment with a promise), so that it may be well with you, and that you may live long on the earth."* This clearly shows that there is a promise from God of long life to those who will honor and obey their parents. Obviously the promise is invalid for the rebellious and disobedient.

If God, in His sovereignty, has already established the time and the manner by which every person will die, we should only see that picture of Divine fate in the Bible. There should be no descriptions of people shortening or lengthening their lifespan on earth by their own choices. Correct? Well, let's see what else the final authority tells us!

> *My son, forget not My law; but let thine heart keep My commandments: for length of days, and long life, and peace, shall they add to thee* (Proverbs 3:1-2).

If you choose to live by God's ways, then peace, long life, and length of days will be added to you.

Hear, O My son, and receive My sayings; and the years of thy life shall be many (Proverbs 4:10).

The fear of the Lord is the beginning of wisdom: and the knowledge of the holy is understanding. For by Me thy days shall be multiplied, and the years of thy life shall be increased (Proverbs 9:10-11).

The fear of the Lord prolongs life, but the years of the wicked will be shortened (Proverbs 10:27 NASB).

Keep God's laws and you will live longer; if you ignore them, you will die (Proverbs 19:16 GNT).

Obey the Lord and you will live a long life, content and safe from harm (Proverbs 19:23 GNT).

Be kind and honest and you will live a long life; others will respect you and treat you fairly (Proverbs 21:21 GNT).

Obey the Lord, be humble, and you will get riches, honor, and a long life (Proverbs 22:4 GNT).

Men of bloodshed and deceit will not live out half their days (Psalm 55:23 NASB).

Some people ruin themselves by their own stupid actions and then blame the Lord (Proverbs 19:3 GNT).

So you can clearly see from Scriptures that our own choices and actions can multiply our days, increase our years, and prolong our lives, or we can shorten our lifespan and ruin our own lives. *"So choose life in order that you may live"* (Deut. 30:19 NASB).

As you are beginning to see, free will is an awesome privilege, but it also carries with it a weight of responsibility. Why would God, in His sovereignty, choose to give individuals the power of choice? Let's go into the next chapter and get some answers!

Chapter 5

WHAT IS LOVE?

"For God, as to His nature, is love" (1 John 4:8 Wuest[1]).

"The World is built for God's love. God is the Great Cosmic Lover.... He is the ultimate Agape.... He loves and wants to be loved by us."[2]

Picture with me a "Stepford wife" type of relationship. The husband has predetermined and preprogrammed exactly how he wants his wife to act and respond toward him. She has no other choice than to do all that her husband wants. She always prepares the kind of food he prefers, and it's always the way that he likes it. She dresses totally to fit his tastes for every occasion. She is always in the perfect mood; no unpredictable mood swings for her! When it comes to romance, she never turns him down and always responds with the right amount of passion. The husband thinks he has the perfect relationship for the first few months, but eventually it loses all meaning. Why? Everything she's doing toward him, *he's* doing! Having programmed her responses, he's simply loving himself. You cannot program genuine love. Love requires freedom of choice.

I once had an "extreme sovereignty" friend tell me that if God had selected a person to be one of His "elect," that person would be saved—period! Since my friend believes that we have no free will or ability to choose, God will force the matter and make it happen. That's really what he told me.

Young lady, what if a young man tried to win you over by force? The doorbell rings, you answer, and a stranger grabs you by the arm and puts a gun to your head saying, "I have selected you to be my bride as long as we both shall live. Come with me!" Would you love that young man? Would you trust and respect him? Would you want to be near him and spend time with him?

Rather, he should try to win you over by showing you his best, right? The doorbell rings, and there stands a handsome man sharply dressed, teeth brushed, freshly shaven, just the right amount of fragrant cologne, offering you a beautiful bouquet. He extends his arm to you and leads you to his clean, polished car. He then proceeds to take you to your favorite restaurant where you enjoy a relaxed meal by candlelight. Of course he picks up the tab! Would you be more favorably inclined toward this young man?

How does God try to reach people on planet Earth? By force or by persuasion?

> ...*The goodness of God leads you to repentance*
> (Romans 2:4 NKJV).

...Don't you know that the reason God is good to you is because He wants you to turn to Him? (Romans 2:4 CEV).

So you see, our love for Him comes as a result of His loving us first (1 John 4:19 LB).

I have loved you with an everlasting love; therefore I have drawn you with lovingkindness (Jeremiah 31:3 NASB).

From these verses, we can see that God endeavors to reach people with His love, goodness, and lovingkindness.

COMPULSION OR PERSUASION?

God "saves by persuasion, not compulsion, for compulsion is no attribute of God."[3] What is meant by *compulsion?* Well, it means coercion, or using force to gain compliance. If you believe that omnicontrol is an attribute of God, then you believe that God meticulously controls everything that you do.

Do you admire a world leader who governs by compulsion? How about Josef Stalin, dictator over the Soviet Union from 1929 to 1953? Historians say he killed about 20 million of his own people in an effort to control everything and everybody. When Stalin entered his assembly hall to meet with hundreds of his leaders, no one wanted to be the first to stop clapping for fear of losing his life. The clapping would continue for 45 minutes. Finally, Stalin decided to ring a bell so that everyone could stop clapping at the same time.

Why would people admiringly say that God exercises omnicontrol over people and yet disdain that quality when they see it in earthly leaders? Do you really believe that God rules by force and that, therefore, you have no choice? We find leaders detestable who try to rule with absolute control—is God a cosmic dictator?

UNDERSTANDING TRUE LOVE

God's plan has always been for humans to align our will with His will; to choose what He desires for us. But because God's nature is love, that alignment could not be forced or preprogrammed. Remember, there were two trees in the Garden of Eden; that obviously speaks of choice (see Gen. 2:9). When God desires a love relationship with us, we must have the freedom to choose or reject His love. "Forcing" someone to love another is a misunderstanding of love.

For free will to really be free, it must be irrevocable. Can God really give me free will and then step in and stop me every time I'm about to use it wrongly? In essence, God tells me, "Choose this day whom you will serve." I say, "OK, I choose to serve satan." God says, "No! No!" I say, "Okay, I choose to serve drugs and alcohol." "No! No!" "OK, I choose to be selfish and serve myself." "No! No!" I say, "I thought You said for me to choose, God?"

So you can see that the potential to go God's way of love carries with it the potential to reject and oppose the way of love. Consequently, God chose to tolerate the evil that wrong choices have brought about! Because of love, God created a world in which His creatures can actually say no to Him;

which, by the way, is what sin is. So then we have a lot of free wills making decisions in the world that are not God's will.

God is pure love, and His will is always good, acceptable, and perfect (see Rom. 12:2). When you choose a will other than God's, what are you choosing to enter into? The opposite of perfect love is selfishness, greed, worry, strife, jealousy, rage, hatred, chaos! Now you can see why countries, politics, workplaces, marriages, and families—the world—is so fouled up!

People, not God, must determine whether or not they will love God and others. This, of course, leaves the door open for evil. When you see an evil intent in the world, it's the result of a will other than God's. Things can happen that are genuinely not God's will when free will is possible. "Free will has made evil possible. Why then did God give free will? Because free will, though it makes evil possible, is also the only thing that makes possible any love or goodness or joy worth having."[4]

Since God wanted creatures who could choose to love Him, the opposite was always a possibility. This explains why God created a world in which evil is possible. We can also see why the world has become a war zone, and the fault goes to humans and angels for misusing their freedom of choice. Before we move on, let me reiterate the point—for love to have true meaning, it must be chosen, which introduces the possibility that it can be rejected.

OPPOSING THE WILL OF GOD

Again, all evil in the world comes from free wills other than God's; God's will is always good, acceptable, and perfect (see Rom. 12:2). God wants His will to be extended through people who choose to cooperate with Him. This is why Jesus taught us to pray, *"Your will be done on earth as it is in heaven"* (Matt. 6:10 NKJV).

The Scriptures make it clear that there are agents who actively try to thwart God's will for people with the intent to keep them out of it. Apostle Paul reported, *"For a great and effective door has opened to me, and there are many adversaries"* (1 Cor. 16:9 NKJV). It's obvious that God opened the door for him and equally obvious that someone other than God was opposing him.

"Therefore we wanted to come to you—even I, Paul, time and again—but Satan hindered us" (1 Thess. 2:18 NKJV). Notice he didn't say, "God, in His sovereign will, kept us from coming." People can keep themselves out of God's will by choosing to go their own way. *"...[Such people] have chosen their own ways, and they delight in their abominations"* (Isa. 66:3 AMP). An abomination is something that is detestable to God.

> *I have spread out My hands all day long to a rebellious people, who walk in the way which is not good, following their own thoughts* (Isaiah 65:2 NASB).

> *But My people would not hearken to My voice, and Israel would have none of Me. So I gave them up to their own hearts' lust and let them go after their own stubborn will, that they might follow their own counsels. Oh, that My people would listen to Me, that Israel would walk in My ways!* (Psalm 81:11-13 AMP)

Could it be any clearer than that? If you stubbornly insist on your own way, God will let you have it, even though He wants you to choose His way. You then, by your own choice, effectively keep yourself out of God's good, acceptable, and perfect will. Years ago a wise, old man said to me, "No greater punishment can any man have than to be left to have his own way." If your way does not line up with God's way, beware of insisting upon it!

CHOICE SETTLES DESTINY

Free will or fate? Choice or no choice? Is our ultimate destiny a result of our own choices, or do we have no choice, with God already having preprogrammed our lives in such a way that we have no choice in the matter?

Why is any of this important? Because what you believe rules you! Your belief system determines what you embrace and accept into your life and what you resist and reject as unacceptable! Wrong beliefs will hold you in bondage and keep you out of God's good pleasure, while believing and choosing the truth will set you free and keep you in liberty (see John 8:32).

Your choices determine to a large degree what you experience in life, what you accomplish—they carry positive or negative consequences. A person is free to choose his or her own moral actions and even his or her eternal destiny. Courts of law have always operated from the basis of judging individuals from the standpoint of people being free moral agents responsible for what they've chosen to do. God, of course, holds people responsible for their choices, and corresponding consequences always follow.

BELIEVERS IN FREE WILL

Justin Martyr (A.D. 100-165) made this clear defense in behalf of free will:

> We have learned from the prophets, and we hold it to be true, that punishments, chastisements, and rewards are rendered according to the merit of each man's actions. Otherwise, if all things happen by fate, then nothing is in our own power. For if it be predestined that one man be good and another man evil, then the first is not deserving of praise or the other to be blamed. Unless humans have the power of avoiding evil and choosing good by free choice, they are not accountable for their actions— whatever they may be.[5]

Clement of Alexandria, whose writings are dated about A.D. 190, confirmed the same belief: "Neither praise nor condemnation, neither rewards nor punishments, are right if the soul does not have the power of choice and avoidance, if evil is involuntary."[6]

Christian martyr Methodius wrote this near the end of the third century: "Those who decide that man does not have free will, but say that he is governed by the unavoidable necessities of fate, are guilty of impiety toward God Himself, making Him out to be the cause and author of human evils."[7]

In A.D. 320 Archelaus wrote, "He gave to every individual the sense of free will, by which standard He also instituted the law of judgment.... There can be no doubt that every individual, in using his own proper power of will, may shape his course in whatever direction he pleases."[8]

I have read that over 4,000 times in Scripture words such as *choose, choice,* or *will* are used to express the power of individual choice. Therefore, we can safely say that God, in His sovereignty, has chosen to give people a free will.

DID GOD MAKE THE DEVIL "A DEVIL"?

Was God responsible for the fall of lucifer? Did God make lucifer to become the epitome of evil in the world? Who is responsible for all the evil in the world? Let's go to the final authority of God's Word to find out what the truth is concerning lucifer and angels.

> *How art thou fallen from heaven, O Lucifer, son of the morning! How art thou cut down to the ground, which didst weaken* [overthrow, prostrate] *the nations!* (Isaiah 14:12)

Two things can be clearly seen here. This angel had a definite fall from a high and exalted position; and there was a weakening or overthrow of the nations.

The next two verses show us how and why he fell.

> *For thou hast said in thine heart, I will ascend into heaven, I will exalt my throne above the stars of God: I will sit also upon the mount of the congregation, in the sides of the north: I will ascend*

> *above the heights of the clouds; I will be like the*
> *most high* (Isaiah 14:13-14).

Notice carefully that lucifer said five times, *"I will."* How could he will anything if there's no such thing as free will?

Once again, I want to take you back to the early church fathers who lived in the second century to see what they had to say on this most important subject.

Irenaeus wrote, "He [Lucifer] apostatized from God of his own free will"[9] He also wrote, "In man, as well as in angels, [God] has placed the power of choice (for angels are rational beings)."[10]

Origen taught that God created lucifer and gave him his being; but lucifer, of his own free will, made himself into that evil one that today is called the devil. Origen said, "It is as if we should say that a murderer is not a work of God, while we may say that in respect he is a man, God made him."[11]

Scripture confirms this view as it refers again to lucifer in Ezekiel 28:14-15:

> *Thou art the anointed cherub that covereth; and*
> *I have set thee so: thou wast upon the holy moun-*
> *tain of God; thou hast walked up and down in the*
> *midst of the stones of fire. Thou wast perfect in thy*
> *ways from the day that thou wast created, till iniq-*
> *uity was found in thee.*

Let's take note of some things from these references in Isaiah and Ezekiel. God created this angelic being, lucifer, and he was perfect in his ways until iniquity was found in him. What was the nature of his iniquity? Lucifer said five times, *"I will ascend into heaven," "I will exalt my throne," "I will sit also upon the mount," "I will ascend," "I will be like the Most High."* In other words, he wanted to exalt himself over the Supreme Ruler, the sovereign God. He did not want to have a God over him; he wanted to be his own god. As I've heard it so aptly said, "His uprising was his downfalling."

Pride is the treason of the creature against its Creator; to want to become a god instead of having a God. God is always true to His own nature and His own ways, so we see Matthew 23:12 enacted upon lucifer: *"Whosoever shall exalt himself shall be abased* [brought low]."

A rebellion against God is a rebellion against love, and the end result is a fall into all that is the opposite of God's perfect love. After rebelling against God, lucifer then became satan—a being who is the source and originator of all evil. Satan is a cosmic Hitler, Stalin, Mao, and Pol Pot rolled into one! As we shall see later, all evil actions on earth have sprung out of this fallen, satanic nature.

Let's sum this all up by saying that God does not value free will for the sake of free will, but for the sake of love. For true love to be a possibility, the choice to hurt, misuse, and abuse must also be a possibility. God supremely and sovereignly rules over the entire universe, but He does not micromanage your every choice, and He does not exercise omnicontrol over those to whom He has given free will.

So who will answer for the evils of this world?

Clement of Alexandria said, "So in no respect is God the author of evil.... Free choice and inclination originate sins."[12]

Origen said, "Evils do not proceed from God."[13]

If we imperfect beings are outraged at all the morally wrong occurrences in life, how much more must be our Creator God, who has made us in His image and who is Himself perfect love.

Currently we can easily see that on planet Earth God's will is not the only will that affects things. The reason our world looks like a war zone between good and evil is because it *is* a war zone between good and evil!

Someday the final end of satan and all evil will be forever settled, and this raging world war will come to a glorious end. *"Yet thou* [satan] *shalt be brought down to hell, to the sides of the pit"* (Isa. 14:15).

God is sovereign, He rules over all, and all that He stands for—love, truth, justice, equity, peace, joy, harmony, and well-being—will ultimately triumph!

Chapter 6

WHERE DID EVERYTHING GO WRONG?

Strange as it may seem, most of us go everywhere attempting to deal with our trouble, except to the very place where things went wrong! How many of us, after having a flat tire, would check in the glove box or look in the radiator to find the problem? *Genesis* means "beginnings," so we are going to have to go back to the beginning to find out what went wrong.

We know from the Bible that God created all things for His pleasure (see Rev. 4:11). We know that He has the heart of a father, and His desire was and is always to have a family that He could shower His love upon (see Eph. 3:14-15; 1 John 3:1). After creating everything that we would ever need, He created us last and placed us in the midst of it.

Picture the preparations you make before your first child comes into the earth. You paint the baby's bedroom and buy the crib, blankets, pajamas, diapers, formula, bottles, pacifiers, toys, lotions—in short, everything that baby will need. You received those parental instincts from the Father heart of God!

Man and woman could enjoy everything in God's entire creation, with the exception of one thing, *"But of the tree of the knowledge of good and evil, thou shalt not eat of it"* (Gen. 2:17). That one tree speaks to us of choice; and we know that love cannot be real unless it can be chosen or refused. Notice this is a tree of the "knowledge of good and evil," not a pear tree or an apple tree or a common fruit tree.

God's perfect plan was to make an incomplete man-woman whose perfect love, sufficiency, and completion was found only in his and her God. It's accurately been said that there's a God-shaped hole in all of us, and until that void is filled with God alone, we remain incomplete and unfulfilled.

The first man and woman believed the biggest lie of the universe, "You don't need God! If you'll get out from under God's hand, you'll be free, independent, and subject to no one. Don't remain dependent upon God; be independent, and you'll be your own god! Choose to determine good and evil, right and wrong, by establishing the fountain of wisdom within yourself. You'll become your own source of wisdom and you won't need God!"

Like sheep to the slaughter, Adam and Eve fell into satan's trap. Thinking they could live a better life without God, they plunged the whole world into darkness and misery. This decision resulted in utter failure, and failure is a life that leaves God out. Now the world was placed into that unenviable position in which *"every man did that which was right in his own eyes"* (Judg. 17:6).

Adam and Eve took the bait and allowed the root of lucifer's own sin, pride, to be planted deep within them. Again, pride is the treason of the creature against its Creator; to become a god instead of having a God. It's been well said that pride was lucifer's undoing and remains the prime means by which he continues to bring about the undoing of men and women.

GOD'S ORIGINAL INTENTION

God created humanity to be His eternal associate and companion. I remember years ago when I was reading the genealogy listed in the Gospel of Luke, that this phrase jumped out at me for the first time, *"Adam, which was the son of God"* (Luke 3:38). Of course "son" is recorded with a small "s." None of us is deity; there is a God and you are not Him. But this phrase served to drive home for me the point that God made us in His image to be His eternal associates.

> We are told in Psalm 8:4-6 (NKJV), *"What is man that You are mindful of him, and the son of man that You visit* [or care for] *him? For You have made him a little lower than the angels, and You have crowned him with glory and honor. You have made him to have dominion over the works of Your hands; You have put all things under his feet."*

Dominion is almost a lost word in the vocabularies of most theologians. Dominion simply means "to have rule over"; and to have "all things put under your feet" means to have complete authority. Notice that this is exactly what God chose to do in the beginning:

> *Then God said, "Let us make man in Our image,*
> *according to Our likeness; let them have dominion*
> *over the fish of the sea, over the birds of the air, and*
> *over the cattle, over all the earth and over every*
> *creeping thing that creeps on the earth." So God*
> *created man in His own image; in the image of*
> *God He created him; male and female He created*
> *them. Then God blessed them, and said to them,*
> *"Be fruitful and multiply; fill the earth and subdue*
> *it; have **dominion** over the fish of the sea, over the*
> *birds of the air, and over every living thing that*
> *moves on the earth"* (Genesis 1:26-28 NKJV).

In verse 26, God says that He will *"let them have domin-*
ion." Can God do that? Absolutely! God, in His sovereignty,
chose to let them have it. In verse 28, God told them to *subdue*
the earth. What does subdue mean? To conquer, master,
control, check, or restrain. Webster defines subdue this way,
"To conquer and bring into subjection."[1] God gave man this
responsibility; and this was not just a suggestion, but an order
from their sovereign, Father God.

What was there that needed to be conquered and brought
into subjection? I'm glad you remembered—satan, the originator of all evil. Adam was given the responsibility to be
over the earth—"the works of God's hands"—and yet still to
be under the mighty hand of God. Adam's Father God was
always to be his Lord.

> *Then the Lord God took the man and put him in*
> *the garden of Eden to tend and **keep it.** And the*

Lord God commanded the man, saying, "Of every tree of the garden you may freely eat; but of the tree of the knowledge of good and evil you shall not eat, for in the day that you eat of it you shall surely die" (Genesis 2:15-17 NKJV).

Notice the phrase in verse 15, *keep it.* That Hebrew word is *shamar*, meaning "to hedge about, guard, protect."[2] Why are guards needed? In some of my world travels I've had to stay in guarded compounds that were surrounded with high walls. The tops of these walls were covered with broken glass, razor wire, barbed wire, etc., for one reason only—to keep out thieves and enemies! Humankind has a responsibility and is accountable for what he allows into the earth. The world's present and future condition and well-being hinges totally upon the stewardship of human beings!

Remember, God has given humanity freedom of choice. If they make the wrong choice, He will allow their choices to stand. Adam decided that he did not want to stay under God's authority, so he yielded to satan's suggestion to be independent and to go his own way. "Don't have a God over you, be your own god and you'll really be free!" Satan seductively hissed. Sadly, Adam bought the biggest lie of the universe and sold himself and all his descendants into a miserable existence of slavery and sorrow. Suddenly, the earth was subjected to that place and condition in history that we call "the Fall," and the result? "Houston—we have a problem!"

Eight times in Genesis 1:26-28 God tells Adam he has dominion over, over, over—and now he's fallen immediately under, under, under *"the dominion of darkness"* (Col.

1:13 NIV). After he took the forbidden fruit and ate of it, the first statement out of Adam's mouth was, "*I was afraid*" (Gen. 3:10). His first son murdered his own brother out of envy (see Gen. 4:8). The plant and vegetable kingdom became infested with thorns, thistles, and weeds (see Gen. 3:18).

Members of the animal kingdom had always lived in peace and harmony on planet Earth; now they became vicious and began to devour one another. I wonder how long it took for Adam to experience his first dog bite? Adam, in effect, committed high treason against God and relinquished his God-entrusted authority and responsibility of planet Earth over to satan! That's a horrible thought to consider, but I will soon show you that the Holy Scriptures give us proof that it's true.

THE HORRIBLE CONSEQUENCES OF ADAM'S FALL

Let's look at what the Fall of Adam brought about:

1. It changed, altered God's original intention.

2. It separated all humanity from God.

3. It brought Adam and all humans to come under the authority and bondage of sin and satan.

4. It gave satan dominion over God's creation.

5. It cursed the earth and turned it into a great battlefield ruled by violence, hatred, fear, greed, deception, disease, and death.

We can clearly say that the Fall and the present conditions of life on planet Earth are neither God's will nor God's fault.

We are told that God considers even death to be an enemy, *"The last enemy that shall be destroyed is death"* (1 Cor. 15:26). All that is evil, destructive, tormenting, confusing, unjust, and cruel heads up in satan. From the cradle to the grave, he seeks to steal, kill, and destroy the human race (see John 10:10). Jesus said of satan, *"He was a murderer from the beginning and…he is a liar and the father of lies"* (John 8:44 NASB).

EVIL GAINED DOMINION OVER THE EARTH

You might say, "Well, I don't know about the statement that Adam gave satan dominion over God's creation."

Before Jesus launched out into ministry, He fasted for 40 days in the wilderness. As He approached the end of His fast, satan assaulted Him with three temptations. Notice what the devil clearly said in temptation number two:

> *Then the devil, taking Him up on a high mountain, showed Him all the kingdoms of the world in a moment of time. And the devil said to Him, "**All this authority** I will give You, and their glory; for this has been **delivered to me,** and I give it to whomever I wish. Therefore, if You will worship before me, all will be Yours"* (Luke 4:5-7 NKJV).

Satan basically said, "All this authority over the kingdoms of the world has been delivered to me!" By whom? Adam! He also said, "And I give it to whomever I wish." Could he? Yes! He could do it just like Adam did it. Luke 4:6 (NEB[3]) puts it this way, *"**All this dominion** will I give to you…for it has been put in my hands and I can give it to anyone I choose."*

If satan did not have dominion and was telling Jesus a lie and Jesus didn't know it, then Jesus was not the Son of God. If that was anything other than the truth, then it was not a true temptation. But sadly it was the truth, and the awful truth is that Adam had legally transferred the dominion of the earth that God had entrusted to him over to satan.

INFALLIBLE PROOFS

Notice what Jesus Himself said about satan having authority over this world. In John 12:31, 14:30, and 16:11, Jesus calls satan the *prince of this world*. The Greek word is *archon,* "to rule, denotes a ruler, a prince."[4]

"I will no longer talk much with you, for the ruler of this world is coming, he has no power over Me" (John 14:30 RSV[5]). And again, *"I shall not be able to talk much longer to you, for the spirit that rules this world is coming very close. He has no hold over Me"* (John 14:30 Phillips[6]).

Jesus was the Son of God, not the Son of Adam, and He's the only One since Adam who was never tripped up by sin. That's why He can confidently say that satan has no power, authority, or dominion over Him.

> *If the Good News that we preach is hidden, it is hidden only to those who are lost.* ***The devil who rules this world*** *has blinded the minds of those who do not believe. They cannot see the light of the Good News—the Good News about the glory of Christ, who is exactly like God* (2 Corinthians 4:3-4 NCV).

In the King James Version, this verse calls satan the *god of this world,* with a lowercase *g*; he is not deity.

"We know [positively] that we are of God, and the whole world [around us] is under the power of the evil one" (1 John 5:19 AMP). People are deceived to think that they are under no one's authority; that's the original lie, "You don't need to be under God, you can be a god unto yourself!" People are either under the authority of God or the evil one. As Bob Dylan so aptly penned it in his song, "It may be the devil or it may be the Lord, but you gotta serve somebody."[7]

People who will use their free choice to turn and come under God's authority by making Jesus their Lord can come safely under the authority and dominion of God! (See Romans 10:9-10 and John 1:12.) As explained in Colossians 1:13 (NIV):

> *For He has rescued us from **the dominion** of darkness and brought us into the kingdom of the Son He loves.*

After Jesus was raised from the dead, His early disciples went all around the world, and they knew that the import of the Good News message was:

> *To open their eyes so that they may turn from darkness to light and **from the dominion of Satan to God,** that they may receive forgiveness of sins and an inheritance among those who have been sanctified by faith in Me* (Acts 26:18 NASB).

So it's very obvious that only one Man can rescue you and get you out from under the rule of darkness—the God-Man, Christ Jesus!

Chapter 7

WHY JESUS?

Who was this Jesus of Nazareth? Some say that He was a great teacher. Some say that He was one of the greatest religious leaders of the world. Who does the Bible say He was, and what does Jesus say about Himself?

Remember these facts: In Genesis 1:26-28 God told Adam, the representative of the human race, to have dominion over everything on the land, sky, and sea. Psalm 8:6 says that God made Adam to have dominion over the works of His hands. Adam was never to have dominion over himself; he was always to remain submitted to the lordship of his Father God. So God in His sovereignty chose to give the human race the responsibility to steward the earth and yet still to be under the mighty hand of God. We were never meant to live apart from God, as if we were God ourselves! We were meant to live in complete dependence upon God, enjoying a life of friendship and intimate fellowship with Him.

But Adam, our representative man, chose to believe the biggest lie of the universe, "Get out from under God's hand

and you'll be free, independent, and subject to no one. Don't remain dependent upon God, be independent and you'll be your own God!" So, the Fall of the human race occurred, and instead of being "over, over, over," they immediately fell "under, under, under."

All who choose to live their lives independent from God are under the "*dominion of darkness*" (Col. 1:13 NIV). This fallen condition has unfortunately affected every human being. The whole world is *under the power of the evil one* (1 John 5:19 AMP). This includes all of the religious leaders of men. Someone, a Rescuer, is going to have to come into the earth who is not under the authority and dominion of the evil one!

HERE COMES JESUS!

The Bible says that Jesus is "*holy, blameless, unstained by sin and separated from sinners*" (Heb. 7:26 AMP) Jesus said:

> ...*the prince (evil genius, ruler) of the world is coming. And he has no claim on Me. [He has nothing in common with Me; there is nothing in Me that belongs to him, and he has no power over Me]* (John 14:30 AMP).

So the whole world, with the exception of this One, is under the dominion of the evil one. How could this be true of Jesus?

All human beings have come out of Adam's seed. We have inherited his fallen position and condition. Jesus did not come into the earth like the rest of us.

Now the birth of Jesus Christ took place under these circumstances: When His mother Mary had been promised in marriage to Joseph, before they come together, she was found to be pregnant [through the power] of the Holy Spirit....Behold the virgin shall become pregnant and give birth to a Son, and they shall call His name Emmanuel—which, when translated, means, God with us....But he [Joseph] had no union with her as her husband until she had borne her firstborn Son; and he called His name Jesus (Matthew 1:18,23,25 AMP).

Jesus did not come into the earth through Adam's seed like all the rest of us. God planted His Seed into the virgin's womb by the power of the Holy Spirit. Father God sent His only begotten Son to be the Savior of the whole world. Everyone else needs a savior except Emmanuel—He *is* the Savior. That's why the virgin birth was a necessity! Christians who say they don't believe in the virgin birth cancel out their faith in Jesus as their Savior. If Jesus came into the earth through Adam's seed, like all other humans, He would have inherited Adam's fallen condition and needed a savior Himself.

JESUS—THE GOD-MAN—IN DOMINION

Jesus comes on the scene and instead of being under the dominion of sickness, sin, and the powers of evil, He constantly exercises dominion over them! Sickness is powerless before Him—He speaks to fevers, commanding them to leave, and they leave. He has power over leprosy, paralysis, deafness, blindness, and dumbness. He exercises dominion over the elements of the earth—the winds and the waves obey Him, He walks on water, He multiplies bread and fish. The people who witnessed those events said, *"Who then is this, that even the wind and the sea obey Him?"* (Mark 4:41 NASB).

Every other person on earth was under the dominion of evil. Jesus was in dominion over all the powers of evil.

> *And they were all so amazed and almost terrified that they kept questioning and demanding one of another, saying, What is this? What new (fresh) teaching! With authority He gives orders even to the unclean spirits and they obey Him!* (Mark 1:27 AMP)

JESUS—THE LAST ADAM

The Bible calls Jesus the last Adam in First Corinthians 15:45. Just as all people who come into the earth and trace their physical life back to the first Adam, all who are born again into the Kingdom of God trace their spiritual life back to the last Adam, Jesus Christ. Not only is Jesus Christ the Head of the new creation family of God, He is also our Pattern Man.

God's family of love has written songs and books for centuries expressing the desire to be like Jesus—and rightly so—but do we really mean it? All new creatures in Christ must operate as the Pattern Man operated. We must faithfully teach what He taught and practice what He practiced to truly "be like Jesus" and represent Him and His message to our generation: *"Whoever claims to live in Him must walk* [live] *as Jesus did"* (1 John 2:6 NIV).

We cannot pick and choose, slice and dice, or cut and paste what we feel is relevant and pertains to us today from Jesus' teachings and practices. Too many of His followers have done this very thing and are presenting a watered-down version of Jesus' gospel. Jesus Christ is the same yesterday, today, and forever, according to Hebrews 13:8. His gospel is called the *"everlasting gospel"* (Rev. 14:6), and no human being has the authority to alter or change any part of it.

UNDER AND OVER

Remember, the first Adam did not want to remain under the authority of Father God. He chose to go his own way and live his life independently from God and His ways. Instead of bringing him into "*freedom,*" this brought him into bondage and placed him "*under*" the power of the evil one (see 1 John 5:19 AMP).

Along comes the last Adam, Jesus, and instead of being "under" diseases, disasters, demons, and death, like the rest of humanity, He is constantly exercising dominion "over" sin, satan, and all the works of the devil. Why? Jesus tells us and shows us how all born-again sons and daughters of God are to relate to the Father and conduct themselves as citizens of His Kingdom.

Jesus, who is and was always God, humbles Himself as our Representative Man and shows us how life is to be lived in relationship to Father God. He lived His life in complete dependence upon and loving submission to His Father God. He clearly tells us this in His own words:

> *I'm telling you this straight. The Son can't independently do a thing, only what He sees the Father doing. What the Father does, the Son does. The Father loves the Son and includes Him in everything He is doing* (John 5:19 MSG).

Jesus refused to act by His own independent discretion. Choosing to move independently from the Father was not an option for Him.

> *I am able to do nothing from Myself [independently, of My own accord—but only as I am taught by God and I get His orders]...* (John 5:30 AMP).

Jesus yielded to the Father's directions, refused to live independently from Him, and constantly cooperated with the Father's ways and will. He was fully convinced that "Father knows best," and that His ways are always good, acceptable, and perfect!

> *...I do not seek or consult My own will...but only the will and pleasure of the Father Who sent Me* (John 5:30 AMP).

Jesus lived His entire life totally "under" (in submission to) the Father; and as a result, He was always in dominion "over" all the works of the evil one. God's power flowed through Jesus perfectly because He was always in perfect submission to His

Father. To exercise authority, you must be under authority, being always careful to say what God says and to do what He shows you to do.

This is how Jesus, the Pattern Man, lived His entire life. If we want to be like Jesus, to live like Jesus, we must follow His pattern. Jesus is the Way, and life was meant to be lived according to the way He established for us. The man or woman in Christ must operate as the Man, Christ, operated.

This is why Jesus never experienced a power failure or a moral failure. He was always one with the Father; always in perfect harmony and agreement with Him. His life was simply an extension of the Father's; that's why He could say, "If you've seen Me, you've seen the Father" (see John 14:9). God will freely flow through a life that is lovingly yielded to Him.

Jesus said:

> ...What I am telling you I do not say of My own authority and of My own accord; but the Father who lives continually in Me does the (His) works (His own miracles, deeds of power) (John 14:10 AMP).

Jesus couldn't make it any clearer. Here's what He's saying, "As I trust and rely on the Father, He speaks through Me and gives Me what to say. As I remain submitted and dependent upon Him, He does His own works of power, His miracles, through Me." This was how the Father was glorified through the life of the Son, and this is how He wants to be glorified through your life, too.

AS IT IS IN HEAVEN

As we've already seen, Jesus' worldview was that an enemy had sown evil, hostility, and destruction into the world and something must be done about it. Jesus came into the world to destroy and undo the damage that these evil entities have caused.

> ...*The reason the Son of God was made manifest (visible) was to undo (destroy, loosen, and dissolve) the works the devil [has done]* (1 John 3:8 AMP).

Jesus and the early church did not at all see this current world system as one in which God's sovereign will was being carried out by everything that happens in life. They were as certain that satan and his demons were trying to carry out their purposes as they were that God and His angels were desirous of carrying out divine purposes; and they saw the cosmic clash that was ongoing between these two kingdoms.

Notice how Jesus taught His followers to pray:

> *In this manner, therefore, pray: Our Father in heaven, hallowed be Your name. Your kingdom come. Your will be done on earth as it is in heaven....And do not lead us into temptation, but deliver us from the evil one. For Yours is the kingdom and the power and the glory forever. Amen* (Matthew 6:9-10,13 NKJV).

Jesus taught us to pray that the Father's name be held high and holy, for His Kingdom to come, and for His will to be established on earth as it is in Heaven. This clearly shows us that the will of God is *not* being done in the earth as the Father desires it to be. This prayer then, is a prayer for change, a change that moves the world from one that does not honor His name, where His will is not done, and where His rule and Kingdom are not established—to a world where God's will is established as it should be. In verse 13 you see the warfare aspect again, "Protect, keep, deliver, us from the evil one," and the trials and hardships that contend against us as we follow Him.

CANNOT BE FOUND

You will never find in Jesus' teachings or practices that Father God has some higher good or greater purpose behind the evil in this world, as if satan and his demons were somehow carrying out a higher, sovereign purpose of God. Jesus waged a total war against evil in this world, and Jesus' viewpoint was that everything that is evil comes from the evil one. We can clearly see that all things are *not* from God, as the extreme sovereignty viewpoint so adamantly teaches.

JESUS KEEPS IT SIMPLE

We should give the same answers to people that Jesus did. Notice the explanation Jesus gave to His disciples to clear up what had been a dilemma to them.

> *And as Jesus passed by, He saw a man which was blind from his birth and His disciples asked Him, saying, Master, who did sin, this man or his parents that he was born blind? Jesus answered,*

> *neither hath this man sinned, nor his parents: but*
> *that the works of God should be manifest in him.*
> *I must work the works of Him that sent me, while*
> *it is day: the night cometh, when no man can work*
> (John 9:1-4).

Jesus then proceeded to heal this blind man. In essence, here's what Jesus said, "I'm here to work the works of God, and God sent Me to destroy the works of the devil. God is the Healer, and satan is ultimately behind the cause. (Notice, there's no mention of this man or his parents being the cause.)

There is no sickness in Heaven. God didn't place it here in the beginning, and He didn't establish more of it when Jesus came to the earth. If God uses sickness as His will, then Jesus would have given it to people rather than taking it away from them! Nowhere in Genesis do we find statements like these, "And on the sixth day, God created sickness and disease. And God said, Let there be cancer, flesh-eating disease, asthma, and arthritis!" On the contrary, we find that a major emphasis of Jesus' mission was to remove and eradicate these things from people.

JESUS ESTABLISHES A SEEK-AND-DESTROY UNIT

Not only did Jesus aggressively come against the works of the devil in people's lives, He quickly delegates His authority and power to others and sends them forth to do the same.

> *When Jesus had called the Twelve together, He*
> *gave them power and authority to drive out all*
> *demons and to cure diseases, and He sent them*

> *out to preach the kingdom of God and to heal*
> *the sick. So they set out and went from village to*
> *village, preaching the gospel and healing people*
> *everywhere* (Luke 9:1-2,6 NIV).

Wherever these 13 went, they were bringing good news to the people and bad news to the demons. Jesus' mission was to seek and save the lost and destroy diseases caused by the devil.

> *After these things the Lord appointed seventy*
> *others also, and sent them two by two before His*
> *face into every city and place where He Himself*
> *was about to go. And to heal the sick there, and*
> *say to them, "The kingdom of God is come near to*
> *you"* (Luke 10:1,9 NKJV).

We can clearly see that this sickness-destroying aspect of the gospel was not simply for Jesus and the apostles. Jesus had an "all hands on deck" attitude; in other words, He was willing to enlist any who would make themselves available!

> *John said to Him, 'Teacher, we saw someone*
> *casting out demons in Your name, and we tried to*
> *prevent him because he was not following us." But*
> *Jesus said, "Do not hinder him, for there is no one*
> *who will perform a miracle in My name, and be*
> *able soon after to speak evil of Me. For he who is*
> *not against us is for us"* (Mark 9:38-40 NASB).

So at this point in time, there were Jesus, the 12, 70 others, plus this unknown man—that's a unit of 84—going from city to city and place to place bringing the good news of the Kingdom and destroying the works of the devil.

TO THE END OF THE AGE

After Jesus was crucified and raised from the dead, He appeared to His disciples and clearly commanded them to go into all the world and make disciples, "*teaching them to observe all things that I have commanded you; and lo, I am with you always, even to the end of the age*" (Matthew 28:20 NKJV).

In other words, "Carry on and continue doing and teaching what I've shown you." What are we to do? Go! What are we to preach? The Kingdom of God is here! How do we establish it? Destroy the works of the devil! Jesus commissioned, equipped, and empowered the early church to continue to do what He had been doing. He has given us His power and authority to proclaim and demonstrate the Kingdom just as they did. We are to be about what Jesus was about and stick to the pattern that He established.

The Kingdom of God is established only as the kingdom of darkness is torn down. Our task is to bring the Kingdom of God to bear in a war zone where it is resisted. We are to aggressively be on the offense to destroy the works of the evil one in people's lives—to see his captives set free! It's a task that we can and must successfully carry out. We are never to accept as coming from God that which Jesus fought as coming from satan. A theology of accepting in resignation that all things come from God's hand of sovereignty—essentially saying that therefore all that happens in life is the will of God—could not be any further from the worldview established by Jesus and the early church.

LET'S RECAP

It should be very clear by now that the "extreme sovereignty view" and the "Jesus worldview" are two very differing views, and in many respects they are opposing views. You may ask the question, "I see that, but does it really matter?"

Yes, it matters a great deal! If you believe that everything that comes into your life is the will of God, you will passively accept everything and resist nothing that comes your way. When evil, calamity, sickness, torment, depression, and oppression try to assail you, instead of aggressively rebuking it, like Jesus did, you'll wonder what purpose God intends for it to have in your life. At that point, you've allowed the devil to establish a foothold in your life.

The Bible clearly teaches us:

- *"Do not give the devil a foothold"* (Ephesians 4:27 NIV).

- *"Resist the devil, and he will flee from you"* (James 4:7 NIV).

- *"You must resist the devil and stay strong in your faith"* (1 Peter 5:9 CEV).

- *"...resist in the evil day, and having done everything, to stand firm"* (Ephesians 6:13 NASB).

Let's follow the Jesus worldview with an aggressive faith that endeavors to establish His will in the earth and a militant resistance to every evil work and attack of the devil! Jesus came into this world and confronted things that were against His Father's will, things that came from the will of our enemy.

You've got to know what's coming from which side, the kingdom of darkness or the Kingdom of light, rather than seeing all that happens in life as somehow being part of God's mysterious plan for the earth. All things do *not* come from God.

In Part II some specific questions will be answered:

- If something is God's will for your life, doesn't it always come to pass automatically?

- Are there certain variables that can affect the will of God in your life?

Part II

WHAT ABOUT...?

Chapter 8

WHAT IS TRUTH?

Pontius Pilate asked Jesus this all-important question, *"What is truth?"* (John 18:38). Has truth been established? Can truth be found? Is it possible for a person to arrive at "The Truth"?

Never before on planet Earth has there been such an onslaught of information bombarding the minds of people with the intent of shaping what they believe—movies, magazines, newspapers, books, radio, television, the Internet, professors, politicians, preachers—the avalanche descends! Brainwashed by public opinion, most people believe what everybody else believes and rarely ever stop to ask why. The world is rushing downstream in the mighty flood of public opinion.

What do you believe, and how do you arrive at what is true? That question is of utmost importance because what we believe rules us. It shapes our values, our habits, and our way of living. It opens or closes the door to the will of God in our life. It determines the amount of grace and help from God that we embrace. We believe and therefore we bow to what we believe! Who and what are we bowing to? Are we bowing to opinions, theories, traditions, superstitions, past experiences, personal preferences, feelings, and fears?

Our choice today is the same as it was in the beginning—in the Garden of Eden. We can choose to trust God and believe that He has given us the Truth and revealed His will for us in His Word. We can choose to believe that God has given us Jesus as the Personification of His heart, His way, His will, and His Truth. We can bow to God, who He is and what He says in His Word and through His Son.

Or we can, in pride, exalt ourselves by choosing to decide what we think is true or false and go it alone. We can choose to believe anything we want, as if we were god. You can reject God and His Truth, thereby forfeiting His grace and help for your life. The choice is yours throughout many situations in an average day. Whatever you believe rules in every area and in every situation of your life—Truth or consequences? It's your choice.

GO WITH GOD

"Well, I want to go God's way. I want to know His will, enjoy His will, and agree with what He says. I want to bow to Him on every issue! I know Truth is in God, but how does He speak and make His will, His way, His Truth known?"

"How can I know the Truth?"

Jesus answers that question.

1. *Through the Written Word.* In John 17:17, Jesus was praying to Father God and He said, *"Your*

Word is Truth." The Bible reveals the beginning of humanity—the reason, the nature, and the destiny of humanity. It reveals who God is, what He's like, how He works, what He's done for you, and how you can enter into His plan, purpose, and destiny for your life.

2. *Through the Word Made Flesh.* Before Jesus came to Earth and became a man, He was known as the Word. *"In the beginning was the one who is called the Word. The Word was with God and was truly God"* (John 1:1 CEV).

Whatever God the Father was, the Word was. The two of them are exactly alike and in full agreement.

> *The Word became a human being* [flesh] *and lived here with us. We saw His true glory, the glory of the only Son of the Father. From Him all the kindness and all the truth of God have come down to us* (John 1:14 CEV).

So we can see and understand that all the Truth of God has been revealed to us in the Person of Jesus Christ. Watch Jesus closely, listen to Him, and you will clearly see the heart of God, the ways of God, and the will of God.

Many people will say, "I can't see God, so how can I know Him?" You can see Jesus, and God the Father sent Jesus so that you could know Him through His Son. We are told in the Bible that God has spoken to us by His Son:

> *In the past God spoke to our forefathers through*
> *the prophets at many times and in various ways,*
> *but in these last days He has spoken to us by His*
> *Son...* (Hebrews 1:1-2 NIV).

It becomes obvious that I can only know and understand the Father and the Son through reading the written Word. I can't understand God by my own logic, analysis, impressions, feelings, or sentiments. I can only know and understand God by His Word. His Word is final authority and reveals to me the ultimate Truth.

This brings me to a wonderful choice: I can let go of my own thoughts and exchange them for the thoughts of God that are revealed to me from the Word of God! As I follow God by bowing to the Truth He shows me from His Word, I enter more and more into His glorious freedom, and I discover and enjoy more of His good, acceptable, and perfect will for my life!

> *...If you continue in My word, then you are*
> *truly disciples of Mine; and you will know the*
> *truth, and the truth will make you free* (John
> 8:31-32 NASB).

LOGIC AND REASON

Logic and reason are what we apply to different branches of knowledge. In the realm of math, "Two plus two equals four," or in the realm of science, "What goes up must come down." When it comes to the realm of the spirit, logic and reason are left on the outside with no way to look in.

God in His love and goodness has not left us on the outside, but has bridged the gap between the spirit realm and the physical realm. He has given us His written Word and His Son in order to reveal to us the thoughts and ways of His unseen, spirit realm. When we reject the revelation that God has given, our only option is to turn philosopher, theorist, or guesser. "Well, let me tell you what I think" or "I really feel this way about that subject."

It seems quite apparent to me that most Americans depend upon their own logic and experience to determine their beliefs. They determine what's true or what the will of God is by what they experience and by their own reasoning. Why is that a dangerous approach to take to life?

WHAT IS PRIMARY?

Primary means that which is first in order, rank, or importance; first in order of sequence or in any series, etc. God has no beginning; He is obviously Primary! *"God is a Spirit,"* and *"No man hath seen God at any time"* (John 4:24; 1:18). God, who is a Spirit and is unseen, has created every-thing physical and everything that is seen. Therefore, that which is spirit and unseen has precedence over all that is physical and seen.

Notice what the Bible says about the Word made flesh (Jesus) regarding these truths. Everything was created by Him. God's Son was before all else, and by Him everything is held together (see Col. 1:16-17). These facts cannot be known to us by way of human logic, reasoning, or experience; they must be revealed to us from God and His Word.

Peter learned this when Jesus told him, *"...this was not **revealed** to you by man, but by My Father in heaven"* (Matt. 16:17 NIV). Paul learned as well that God wants to reveal to us things from that wonderful unseen realm of the spirit! *"I did not receive it from any man, nor was I taught it; rather I received it by **revelation** from Jesus Christ"* (Gal. 1:12 NIV).

Think this through with me now. The word *reveal* simply means to uncover or to unveil. How could we know about the acts of God, the ways of God, the will of God, or the character of God without God uncovering these things to us? How could we know who Jesus is, why He came, what happened on the cross and at the resurrection, and what all of it means for us personally unless God had a way of revealing it to us?

Since God has lifted the veil for us by giving us His Word, we can now know the future glory and eternal bliss that awaits each believer. We can now know about the holy angels of God and how they cooperate with God to help every believer. We can know about satan, the fallen angels, and evil spirits. We do not have to continually walk into our enemy's traps because the Bible gives us insight into his evil schemes!

TWO REALMS OF EXISTENCE

> *By faith we understand that the universe was created by the word of God, so that which is seen was not made out of things that are visible* (Hebrews 11:3 ESV[1]).

God has revealed some important facts to us here! Notice carefully that there are two realms of existence. In one realm there are things that are seen and visible. In the other realm there are things that are unseen and invisible. We have a tendency to think that if something cannot be seen, it is nonexistent. But here it states that everything that is seen and visible owes its existence to things that are unseen and invisible.

So I ask you, which realm is primary and foundational? That's right, the spirit realm! The good news is that the things in the seen and physical realm are temporary and subject to change, while the things in God's unseen and spirit realm are solid and eternal! *"…For the things which are seen are temporary, but the things which are not seen are eternal"* (2 Cor. 4:18 NKJV).

So which realm should you anchor your faith in, and which realm should your beliefs be built upon? Jesus said, *"Sky and earth will pass away, but My words will not pass away"* (Matt. 24:35 AMP). We can see that it's not safe to build your faith on the physical realm; nothing there is primary or lasting. It's unwise to say, "I will only believe what I can see or feel!" Everything in that realm is always subject to change and will eventually pass away!

THE UNSEEN REALM

There is a real realm of God that Jesus came to reveal to us called "the Kingdom of God." This realm is a higher realm than the physical realm. Indeed, it's the highest realm of authority. The real things of the Kingdom of God are all spirit.

- God Himself is a Spirit (see John 4:24)

- His Words are spirit; they are living and active (see John 6:63; Hebrews 4:12 NASB).

- His angels are spirits (see Hebrews 1:14).

- In order to enter the Kingdom of God your human spirit must be born of the Holy Spirit (see John 3:6).

- Then you worship God in spirit (see John 4:24).

- You learn to be led by the Spirit (see Romans 8:14).

- You become empowered by the Spirit (see Acts 1:8).

- You receive the gifts of the Spirit (see 1 Corinthians 12:7).

- You develop the fruit of the Spirit (see Galatians 5:22-23).

- You have a live-in Helper and Tutor, the Holy Spirit, who will teach you and guide you into all truth about God, Jesus, and the things of the Kingdom. He will communicate to you Spirit to spirit (see John 16:13-15).

You can see, then, that for a true follower of Jesus Christ, the primary realm is spirit, spirit, spirit! The spirit realm of God determines truth for us. We bow to God's Word, confidently knowing that His Word is reality. His Word is eternal and unchangeable, the most solid thing that anyone can build their beliefs upon. *"Forever, O Lord, Your Word stands firm in heaven"* (Ps. 119:89 NLT). We can live confidently by putting our faith in the unseen and spirit things of God and His Word! Men and women in the Bible have clearly set this example before us. We can safely follow in their footsteps.

> *It was by faith that Moses left the land of Egypt. He was not afraid of the king. Moses kept right on going because he kept his eyes on the One who is invisible* (Hebrews 11:27 NLT).

MAKE THIS TRANSITION

We must all make the transition from basing our lives upon our logic, reason, feelings, and experiences over to Jesus and the Word of God. What we can see or feel at any given time does not determine finality! Here's what I mean: Before Jesus went to the cross and was raised from the dead, He clearly explained to His disciples that this was the plan of God, and it must surely happen. On three separate occasions, He gave them His Word that this was the will of Father God.

"And He began to teach them that the Son of Man must suffer many things...and be killed, and after three days rise again" (Mark 8:31 NKJV). Pretty clear, huh? Yet none of the apostles chose to take Him at His Word and believe Him.

Why? Perhaps it didn't fit their preconceived beliefs about what would happen to the Messiah? Jesus made one thing very clear—we are to take His Word and believe it over what we think, see, feel, or experience!

THE THOMAS SYNDROME

Before we take a close look at the Thomas Syndrome, let's remember that all the other apostles got rebuked for their faulty belief systems as well!

> ...He rebuked their unbelief and hardness of heart, because they did not believe those who had seen Him after He had risen (Mark 16:14 NKJV).

So let's not be too hard on Thomas. We have all made the same wrong choice, one way or another, that Thomas made that day.

> But Thomas, called the Twin, one of the Twelve, was not with them when Jesus came; so the other disciples told him, "We have seen the Lord." But he replied, "Unless I **see** in His hand the print of nails, and put my **finger** in the mark of the nails and thrust my **hand** into His side, **I will not** believe." A week later His disciples were again indoors and Thomas with them. Though the doors were shut, Jesus came and stood among them and said, "Peace to you." He then spoke to Thomas, "Reach your finger here and see My hands; reach and thrust your hand into My

side; do not be faithless, but believe." Thomas
answered Him, "My Lord and my God!" Jesus
said to him, "You have believed because you
have seen Me. Blessed are those who do not see
and yet believe" (John 20:24-29 NBV[2]).

Thomas clearly said, "Unless I see and feel, I will not believe!" Notice, this is an act of his will; it's where he fixes his choice. Seeing, feeling, and experience is his final authority—it's what determines reality to him. Unbelief honors the physical realm as superior to the spiritual realm—it's anchored to the physical—what can be seen and felt.

Faith is anchored to the unseen and spiritual realm and honors God and His Word above the physical realm. Faith does not rely on sight for its confident belief! Most people live their lives thinking that the physical is the primary, superior realm of reality—just like Thomas! But the unseen, spirit realm is the primary, superior reality, and it has power, influence over, and the ability to change and alter the physical realm.

"Too many people are feelings ruled, senses schooled, and devil fooled." I heard that saying years ago and never forgot it. What was satan trying to do in Thomas' life here? He was trying to derail him—to keep him out of the will of God. Thomas was agreeing with satan by going with what he could see and feel. Every time you agree with the devil, you disagree with God. You empower satan and give him permission to move you away from and out of the will of God.

What does it take in order to be saved and enter into the Kingdom of God? A commitment of your life, a confession that Jesus is your Lord, and a belief in your heart that God has raised Him from the dead (see Rom. 10:9-10). Notice that Thomas made that choice, *"My Lord and my God!"* and he finally believed that God had raised Jesus from the dead.

Jesus said, *"Blessed are those who do **not see** and yet believe."* Believe what? Believe that Jesus is Lord and has been raised from the dead! Thomas could have chosen to believe Jesus and His Word without ever seeing or feeling Him!

How do you know Jesus has been raised from the dead? You've chosen to believe God and His Word. How do you know that Jesus is Lord? You've chosen to believe God and His Word. Just because you didn't see it or feel it doesn't mean it didn't happen or doesn't exist.

Who told you it didn't happen? Your feelings? Your logic and reason? Evil spirits? Your limited experiences in life? On what are you building your belief system? Don't let feelings, circumstances, or experiences determine or alter what you believe!

DETERMINE YOUR OWN PRIMARY

Earlier we saw that "primary" means first in order of sequence, rank, or importance. When we apply this to what we believe, our primary is our number one—our starting point—our foundation. Most Americans today depend upon their logic and experiences to formulate what they believe. It's as if people are saying, "This is what I've experienced, so reason tells me that this must be the will of God, the truth, and primary for me. Reason tells me that experience is the best teacher, that seeing is believing, and so I am going to lean to my own understanding and be true to my own feelings." But Jesus clearly asks all of us, *"…Why do you reason about these things in your hearts?"* (Mark 2:8 NKJV).

People rely on and put their confidence in their own reason rather than the Word of God. Reason wants to be first and primary, but why would we ever challenge God's wisdom with our own? The very first reasoning question in the Bible came from the devil, who challenged God's wisdom by asking, *"Has God said?"* (Gen. 3:1).

We can't exalt reason over the revelation that comes only from God's Word. We are told *not* to lean on our own understanding (see Prov. 3:5). This is a dangerous option that we all face, and it will always lead us away from the will of God for our lives!

> *But I fear, lest somehow, as the serpent deceived Eve by his craftiness, so your minds may be corrupted* [led astray] *from the simplicity that is in Christ* (2 Corinthians 11:3 NKJV and NASB).

If the lordship of Jesus Christ means anything to you, it must mean that you rely on and submit to the person of Jesus Christ and the authority of His Word. God's realm—the unseen and spirit realm—is what determines your primary, your starting point, and your foundation. God's realm carries the higher authority, and His Word is what determines finality in your life.

We must always guard our hearts by taking into account the fact that we live in an analytical society that chooses to exalt the intellect and make it good and primary. May God establish in all of us this same commitment, "Though *I* think differently, I will not question Your Word. I will simply believe it because *You* said it. I will not psychoanalyze this situation or give *my* opinion on it. I will simply believe and obey what *You* say about it."[3]

OF WHICH MIND ARE YOU?

Years ago I heard this statement made, "Where the mind goes, the man follows." Is that true, and can it be validated by the Word of God?

> *For those who live according to the flesh set their minds on the things of the flesh, but those who live according to the Spirit set their minds on the things of the Spirit* (Romans 8:5 RSV).

We can safely say that if you're living according to the flesh, your mind is ruled by fleshly and physical thoughts; and if you're living according to the Spirit, your mind is ruled by spiritual and God thoughts.

Jesus said, *"It is the Spirit who gives life; the flesh profits nothing; the words that I have spoken to you are spirit and are life"* (John 6:63 NASB). God's very words are Spirit, and they reveal to us the higher realm of God. His words are Truth, and they reveal to us the character of God, the ways of God, and the will of God in all the issues and affairs of life. God's Word is absolutely primary—first, foundational, our starting point—and His words are Spirit. If we are to be Spirit-minded and Spirit-ruled, our first priority that determines reality and truth will be the Word and Spirit; our second will be faith in the Word and Spirit. Faith in the

Word and Spirit enables the will of God to be made manifest in our experiences in the physical realm, which is our third priority.

So the *Spirit-minded person* builds his or her belief system like this:

1. God's Word reveals His will and truth.

2. I anchor and establish my faith in my first priority (His Word is His will).

3. His Word is then made manifest in the physical realm of my experiences.

Remember the Thomas Syndrome? Unfortunately, that's how most people have built their belief system. "What I see, feel, and experience determines what I believe. That is first, primary for me. Whatever happens or manifests in the physical, flesh realm must be the will of God. My faith is established in the physical, flesh realm—what I can see, feel, and experience determines the will of God in any and every situation. Reason tells me that it has to agree with my experiences to be true. How could it be otherwise? If something is happening in the physical realm, it must be the will of God. So my first priority, my starting point, is the flesh, physical realm."

So the *fleshly minded person* builds his or her belief system like this:

1. Physical experiences and reason determine God's will, truth.

2. I anchor and establish my faith in my first priority (experiences reveal His will).

3. Whatever happens in life I accept as the will of God.

AN EVALUATION

Let me ask you some questions. Do you determine the will of God by your experiences? Do you live your life by "seeing is believing" or "believing is seeing"? Most people subconsciously think that everything has to agree with their experiences or it's not true. "If this were not the will of God, it would not be happening to me." That is a false assumption!

Your perspective of truth must change to fit God's perspective of truth, which can only be known through His Word—His Word is truth. Don't dumb down the standards set by Jesus and His Word and lower it to the level of your current experience. Raise your belief system to the standards of Jesus and His Kingdom. He is to be your primary, your first priority, your final authority. Jesus is our only trustworthy, unshakeable Pattern Man. Learn to know His ways and His will. He alone is the Truth!

You may ask, "But what happened in this situation?" "What about this?" "What about that?" "If something is clearly seen to be the will of God, doesn't the will of God always have to come to pass in a person's life?" "Isn't the will of God always automatic?"

Let's jump ahead and get some answers to those questions.

Chapter 9

VARIABLES?

What is a variable? Something that is "apt to vary, change-able; capable of being varied, alterable."[1] Many people believe that if something is God's will for people, it will happen, period—automatically. *False.* They fail to consider other factors. We are in the midst of hostiles, cosmic terror-ists, who want to enforce their will on people. We live in a continual spiritual war that never lets up! All of our choices, actions, words, and decisions vary and can open up our lives to the things of God or the things of our enemy. God wants peace and goodwill toward you; your enemy wants confusion and ill will toward you. There is no meeting ground between the two. One is the kingdom of darkness and the other is the Kingdom of Light. There is no admixture between the two. God does not jump camps and work sometimes with the devil. He is not a co-laborer together with the devil!

So I ask these questions: Why do many Christians believe and speak like they don't know this? How do we get God mixed up with the works and schemes of the devil?

Apostle Paul instructed his students (and us as well) regarding the difference between the plans of God for your life and the plans of satan. *"So that no advantage would be taken of us by Satan, for we are not ignorant of his schemes"* (2 Cor. 2:11 NASB). It's obvious that if you don't know what's coming at you from satan, your lack of knowledge will allow him to work in your life and take advantage of you! You can now see why God has to make statements like the following, which are sad, but true!

> *My people are destroyed for lack of knowledge...* (Hosea 4:6).

> *Therefore My people have gone into captivity, because they have no knowledge...* (Isaiah 5:13 NKJV).

It's not God's will for His people to live in captivity and bondage, experiencing works of destruction in their lives!

We have seen that the "extreme sovereignty" belief system is based upon a faulty premise that says, "Everything that happens in life is God's will." *False.* That insults the character of God, ignores the fact that we have an adversary, makes God's will equal to that of the devil's, and disarms the Church, which is to aggressively confront the works of the devil and advance the Kingdom of God on the earth.

If you believe that everything in life comes from God, there will be times when you mistakenly embrace situations sent by the devil, thinking that they are sent from God. Then you will wonder and say, "Why is God doing this to me?" I want to clue you in on a fact—He's not! Never agree that

God is behind evil. The devil is allowed to have his way when people ignorantly and unknowingly agree with him! Always remember that satan hates you and has a destructive plan for your life.

PRAYER CHANGES THINGS—REALLY?

Do you really believe that prayer matters? Can prayer alter things in this physical realm and shift things into the will and purpose of God? Do you believe the "extreme sovereignty" view of fate that teaches that whatever God has predetermined for your life, good or evil, will always come to pass? "*Que sera, sera*; whatever will be, will be" is *false*.

If prayer changes things, then we can rightly say that things that could have been changed, won't be changed if we don't pray! We have an awesome opportunity and responsibility to alter and change evil situations if we will pray.

God says in Ezekiel 22:30 that He looked for a man to stand in the gap and pray and intercede for the land to divert destruction. The will of God can be put into effect by one praying person! Nations have been spared and revolutionized by prayer. It was said during World War II that England was saved by a league of praying women.

In Exodus 17:8-16 we have a case in point, where the enemy Amalekite army comes against God's people to destroy them. This battle was fought in a valley, in a real blood and guts, *Braveheart* style of fighting! Moses went on top of a hill overlooking the battle and lifted up his hands as an intercessor. As long as his hands were up, God's people prevailed. Whenever he put his hands down to rest, the enemy prevailed.

Is this a case in which their victory would come unconditionally and the will of God was automatic? Not at all!
Aaron and Hur, two of Moses' assistants, ran to Moses' aid
and supported his arms until sundown. Only until then was
the enemy's will defeated and the victory secured. In honor to
God for bringing His will to pass for His people, Moses built
an altar and called it, "The Lord is my [victory] banner." If
you want to go forward in victory and see the will of the Lord
prevail in your life, keep on praying!

Jesus taught us the necessity of prevailing in prayer until
the will of God manifests by making this statement in Luke
18:1 (NIV), *"Then Jesus told His disciples a parable to show
them that they should always pray and not give up."* Prayer is a
crucial factor that can affect the will of God. Failure to pray
can forfeit the will of God.

Some people don't want any responsibility, neglect the
privilege of prayer, and are run over by the devil! Satan would
rather see you do anything than pray—stay too busy with
work, ministry, computers, television, video games, hobbies,
sports, anything but prayer.

Will there be opposition to prayer? To the will of God
coming to pass? Yes! What do you do? Persevere! Don't quit!
Press through! Win the wrestling match! As stated in Ephesians 6:10-13 (MSG):

> *And that about wraps it up. God is strong, and He
> wants you strong. So take everything the Master
> has set out for you, well-made weapons of the best
> materials. And put them to use so you will be able
> to stand up to everything the Devil throws your*

way. This is no afternoon athletic contest that we'll walk away from and forget about in a couple of hours. This is for keeps, a life-or-death fight to the finish against the Devil and all his angels. Be prepared. You're up against far more than you can handle on your own. Take all the help you can get, every weapon God has issued, so that when it's all over but the shouting you'll still be on your feet....

This is the reality, the way it really is. Will you just ignore the attacks of the enemy and the evil being perpetrated by evil spirits in this world? Will you falsely believe that everything that happens in life is somehow God's sovereign will and settle down into a shell of passivity?

Or will you rise up with your faith in God and be a warrior, a freedom fighter for the sake of the Kingdom of God? Of course, the choice is always yours. Take these words of the prophet to heart, *"Be strong, alert, courageous...and work! For I am with you, says the Lord of hosts"* (Haggai 2:4 AMP).

IS GOD GOOD—OR NOT?

"...No one is good except God alone" (Mark 10:18 NASB). That statement was made by the greatest Teacher ever to grace planet Earth—Jesus Christ. The only Being in existence who is perfectly good is God. We should always expect perfect goodness from Him and nothing else! *"Oh, taste and see that the Lord is good; blessed is the man who trusts in Him!"* (Ps. 34:8 NKJV).

Everything hangs on what you believe about the character of God. Is He perfectly good? Can you really trust Him? Maybe He's not as good as you thought—as loving as you thought? Satan said to our first parents in Genesis 3:1 (NKJV), *"Has God indeed said?"* If Adam and Eve, living in the perfect environment of Eden, could question and doubt God's goodness, is it any wonder that people do today?

If you mistrust who God really is and what He's really like, then that will always place seeds of doubt in your heart about what He says in His Word concerning His will for you. Doubt is the inevitable outcome of mistrusting God's character.

GOD IS GOOD—LIKE JESUS!

- God is who Jesus reveals Him to be. God is like Jesus Christ.

- Jesus is the visible expression of the invisible God (see Colossians 1:15).

- Jesus is the flawless expression of the nature of God (see Hebrews 1:3).

- Jesus said, *"Anyone who has seen Me has seen the Father"* (John 14:9 NLT).

The character and will of God is Jesus Christ, for all time—no what ifs, yeah buts, or maybes! Jesus is what God thinks of people; how God treats people. Jesus is what God thinks of sin, sickness, heartache, and pain. What Jesus wanted people to have is what God wants people to have *today!* Jesus is the will of God for all time.

Experience is not the best teacher—Jesus and His Word are! Don't look at this dysfunctional, evil world or its tragic experiences to determine what God is like or what His will is for people! Too many people have accepted a theology of failure based upon the tragic experiences of life! If you believe that God controls everything that happens in the world, then you are going to have to believe that there is no such thing as evil because God is always good.

Some people mistakenly say, "Well, satan is evil and he's doing the bad, but God is good for having him do it, and somehow all the bad in the world is really producing good results." That's crazy! That's like saying you believe in a round triangle. If you have any degree of this view of God in you, at some level you will always mistrust God. Faith is about completely and accurately trusting the character of God.

NIGHTMARISH OCCURRENCES

I want to be brutally clear by giving you some real experiences to think about. I know you may be able to fill up the next few pages by giving your own similar experiences. My only purpose is to help bring some greater clarity to these very important issues of life.

When I was a little boy, I used to regularly spend the weekends with my grandparents in Arkansas City, Kansas. The family next door had two children about my age, and we always played games outside and had a great time together. One summer day I heard sirens and saw red lights at the house next door. There had been a terrible accident. The little girl had been shot in the face and had died instantly in a gun cleaning accident.

I remember reading an eye-witness account of the war in Kosovo. The journalist reported how heart-sickened he was when he saw toddler girls who had been raped by enemy soldiers. He also said he came upon a scene where some soldiers were playing soccer with the decapitated heads of their enemies.

Now I ask you, are these things the sovereign will of a God who is perfectly good? The Bible says many times that God is love. Where is the love in these types of atrocious acts? So many people have their pat answers that they always fall back on, but the bottom line is that God has nothing to do with such horrific evil. Either you place the responsibility *all* on God or you realize that there are other factors involved in God's will coming to pass in people's lives—free will, choices, decisions, and demonic strategies designed to oppose, confuse, and frustrate you and prevent you from entering into God's will. How we respond or fail to respond to God or the devil makes a difference and affects the outcome. As we've already discussed, whether we pray or don't pray makes a difference!

WWJD?[2]

If Jesus would have nothing to do with toddlers being raped, soccer being played with human heads, and children dying in shotgun accidents, then neither would God the Father. You never see a situation in the Bible in which Jesus comes upon unfortunate victims and tells them some of the pat answers that we commonly hear today. "Well, you're just going to have to endure your suffering; God is sovereign and He has some hidden reason behind your predicament."

Can you picture Jesus coming upon a sick person and saying, "It's not in God's sovereign will to heal you. He's doing a deeper work in your life, and you're actually going to be better off by keeping this condition for the rest of your life. It's a tool of God to help make you holy." Not one time does Jesus tell anyone anything that remotely resembles those statements!

Once again, I want to remind you that most people's starting point, their first priority, is their experiences. Then, they try to reason out and understand their experiences, and that becomes their second priority. They then determine what they think is the will of God, their third priority, from working with their experiences and reason.

Where is Jesus and His Word in all of this? We are to *start* with Jesus and His Word, gain our understanding and put our faith there, *and then* see the will of God come to pass and change the evil situation. That is to always be our one, two, three progression! It actually is always a good practice to ask yourself, "What would the Jesus I know from the Bible do in this situation?" Let's not try to conform Jesus into an image that fits our own reason and logic! Let's let Jesus conform us into *His* unchangeable image.

JEKYLL AND HYDE?

Do you remember the fictional character Dr. Jekyll? He was plagued by a dual personality; one side that was good and the other bad. Does your image of God have a dark side? Does He work in harmony with the devil? Are they co-laborers together? Who is God and who is satan?

There's a world of difference between the two; and just as the kingdom of satan fights against the Kingdom of God, the Kingdom of God should be fighting against the kingdom of satan. Do you really think God conspires with satan and works on both sides? General Sherman said, "War is hell." War is dysfunctional; it's crazy, violent, and hostile. Don't fret and worry about evil. Don't just sit and philosophize about it.

Rise up with your faith in Jesus and do something about it—come against it! For those among us who choose not to, I wonder if they're not convinced or really aware of how much God is against evil in this world. Some people say, "Well, it makes me feel very secure that all comes from God." Yes, and very passive and prayerless; and it's really a very pathetic view of God. There is a real battle going on. There's a real difference between God and satan. God is good all the time. Satan is evil all the time.

None of this matters in the blueprint view of extreme sovereignty. That view tarnishes the character of God, which breaks down your trust in God and builds passivity into you so that your response is dropped and negated. Instead of resisting the works of the devil, you embrace and accept them as somehow being in the sovereign will of God.

IT MATTERS *HOW* YOU PRAY

"Well, I prayed and nothing changed—nothing happened. Therefore, it must not have been the will of God to answer my prayer." Are you sure? How did you pray? It makes a difference *how* you pray!

> *But if any of you lacks wisdom, let him ask of God, who gives to all generously and without reproach, and it will be given to him.* **But** *he* **must** *ask in* **faith** *without any doubting, for the one who doubts is like the surf of the sea, driven and tossed by the wind. For that man ought not to expect that he will receive anything from the Lord, being a double-minded man, unstable in all his ways* (James 1:5-8 NASB).

Here we clearly see that in order to receive the will of God (wisdom, in this case), we must pray and ask for it. But if we don't pray in faith, we won't receive it even though it's the will of God for us to have it! This is true for the will of God in every category of your personal life. If you don't pray in faith, don't expect to receive anything from the Lord.

The Word of God and the Person of Jesus clearly show us what the will of God is for people. If I doubt what they reveal to me about the will of God, I fall into the category of being a double-minded man. I'm like the little girl who pulls a daisy and begins to pluck its petals saying, "He loves me, he loves me not, he loves me, he loves me not..."

Let's look at a clear Bible example.

> *"Is any one of you sick? He should call the elders of the church to pray over him and anoint him with oil in the name of the Lord. And the prayer offered in* **faith** *will make the sick person well; and the*

Lord will raise him up. If he has sinned, he will be forgiven. Therefore confess your sins to each other and pray for each other so that you may be healed... (James 5:14-16 NIV).

In verse 15 it clearly says that the person who has sinned will be forgiven. Would anyone read this portion of Scripture and think that God might not want to forgive people of their sins? No, of course not, because God's Word reveals His will. Faith begins where the will of God is known. So you can confidently pray in faith and receive forgiveness.

This same portion of Scripture says to pray for each other so that you may be healed and that the prayer offered in faith will make the sick person well. The same God who wants you to have forgiveness of your sins wants you to have healing for your body. Many of us have been taught in our churches that this is not true, but if you'd never read the Bible or been to church and you read this for the first time, you would clearly see that God is just as willing to heal sickness as forgive sin.

Remember, there is no other gospel truth than what Jesus brought us, so I refer us to Him as the highest court of appeal. After Jesus healed a paralyzed man, He asked this question, *"Which is easier, to say, 'Your sins are forgiven you,' or to say, 'Arise and walk'?"* (Matt. 9:5 NKJV). Both forgiveness and healing have always been God's will for us. That's God's Good News for us! The psalmist David exhorted us to bless the Lord because He forgives all our sins and heals all our diseases. These are called "benefits" by David and are part of His gracious will for all of us (see Ps. 103:1-3).

Let's go back to James 5:15 (NIV) where it says, "*The prayer offered in faith will make the sick person well.*" If someone came to you and said, "I'm praying that God will forgive me, if it be His will," you would have to help that person correct his or her thinking and praying. When you pray "the prayer of faith," you believe you receive forgiveness right when you pray. (See Mark 11:22 and 24.)

The same can be said about praying "the prayer of faith" for healing—you believe you receive healing right when you pray. So many people pray amiss when it comes to healing. They pray, "Father, if it be Thy will, heal me, and if not…?" That shows that they are not sure if God wants to heal them, which kicks them over into the state of being "double-minded."

Remember, James already told us that when we are double-minded, we are not to expect to receive anything from the Lord. This is truly a variable that affects the will of God in our lives! (See James 1:7-8.)

People invariably ask this question, "Didn't Jesus teach us to pray, 'If it be Thy will?'" Jesus never prayed that way, not even one time, over any of the sick people He healed. If He wanted us to pray for the sick like that, we would see Him doing it in the Bible!

On the contrary, Jesus prayed and spoke in faith over the sick, confidently knowing it was Father God's will for them to be made well. That's a big part of the Good News, the gospel of Jesus Christ. In fact, we see Jesus pray the "If it be Thy will" prayer only one time in the Bible. Before He was to go to the cross and take upon Himself the sin of the whole world, He prayed, *"Father, if it is Your will, take this cup away from Me; nevertheless, not My will, but Yours, be done"* (Luke 22:42 NKJV).

Some call this the prayer of consecration—the devotion and dedication of a person to the will of God. For instance, if you felt in your heart that God was calling you as a missionary to India, you might pray, "Father, I would miss my family, friends, and comfort here in the U.S.; nevertheless, if You're compelling me to go to India, not my will, but Yours be done."

So when certain things are clearly stated in the Bible to be God's will for us, we don't negate them by praying, "If it be Thy will." We confidently receive God's gracious will by praying the prayer of faith—believing we receive our answers right when we pray. When it comes to the will of God for your life, prayer makes a difference—not only *how* you pray, but also *whether* you pray. *"You do not have, because you do not ask [God]"* (James 4:2 NKJV).

WHAT WE KNOW

1. Everything that comes to us in life is not the will of God.

2. God is good all the time, and His will is good, acceptable, and perfect.

3. The character and purpose of God is seen in Jesus Christ. He is *for* good and *against* evil. WWJD?

4. The will of God does not come to pass automatically in people's lives.

5. Prayer affects the will of God for your life—not just *whether* you pray, but *how* you pray.

Chapter 10

DO OUR ACTIONS REALLY MATTER?

Some people believe that if something is God's will for your life, it will always come to pass unconditionally—what you do or say makes no difference and has no effect upon the outcome. Is that a truth that can be verified in the Bible?

DON'T OPEN PANDORA'S BOX

In Greek mythology, Pandora was the first woman. According to the myth, she was given a large box and warned not to open it under any circumstance. She opened this box, which contained all the evils known to humanity, including plagues and diseases, not as a malicious act, but simply out of curiosity. Is there a Bible counterpart—a Pandora's Box—that can open up our lives to every evil thing?

Pay careful attention to the following words:

> *But if ye have bitter envying and strife in your hearts, glory not, and lie not against the truth. This wisdom descended not from above, but is*

> *earthly, sensual, devilish. For where envying and*
> *strife is, there is confusion and every evil work*
> (James 3:14-16).

In the Kingdom of God there is righteousness, peace, and joy, whereas in the kingdom of darkness there is envying, strife, and every evil work!

Envy is simply a resentful awareness of an advantage enjoyed by another, coupled with an unhealthy desire to possess that same advantage. Strife can be an act of contention; or it can simply mean to fight, argue, or bitterly struggle over something.[1]

Is this wisdom to handle things in a spirit of envy and strife? Some Christians think that this is the way to handle things—they think it's OK. *"After all,"* they say, *"it's only natural to strive, fight, and argue."* They forget the truth that God gives us in verse 15, "This wisdom...is earthly, sensual, devilish." In other words, it's demonic (belongs to evil spirits) and it's sensual (of the senses). Remember this quote from Chapter 8, "Too many Christians are senses schooled, feelings ruled, and devil fooled." This is a prime example of the truth behind that statement!

Whenever we choose to go with our feelings, for example, give someone a piece of our mind, and enter into strife, we are opening the door for confusion and *"every evil work"* to enter in! Can you afford to release that into your life? How about turning that loose upon your family?

KILL THOSE SNAKES!

Picture an enemy coming to your door with a gift. He rings the doorbell, opens the box, and runs away. You open the door, and out of the box slithers a king cobra, a black mamba, a coral snake, a rattlesnake, an anaconda, and a python. Would you take a shovel, a baseball bat, or any weapon you could find and beat these dangerous creatures off of your domain? Or would you say, "You know, that's OK, God's grace will still protect me if I let them in."

You might say, "Well, you know, I don't believe that regularly living in envy and strife can bring confusion and every evil work. Every evil work? That's got to be an exaggeration!"

My friend, God does not exaggerate. How long a list would we have if we placed on it *every evil work*? We would have to include confusion, depression, disorder, dysfunction, lack of peace, anxiety, anger, deception, betrayal, mistrust, abuse, bitterness, sickness, disease, financial lack, and continual attacks by evil spirits of every kind. None of these things are the will of God, but what you tolerate will dominate in your life, your family, and your church. Don't open Pandora's Box!

THE ROOT OF STRIFE AND QUARRELING

Only by pride cometh contention: but with the well advised is wisdom (Proverbs 13:10)

Contention is another way of saying strife or quarreling. Our pride is the only way that contention can come in. You are "well advised" if you choose to respond in love. God's love in our hearts is *"patient and kind. Love is not...proud"* (1 Cor. 13:4 NLT). Don't let strife and pride root itself into your life!

"*By insolence the heedless make strife, but with those who take advice is wisdom*" (Prov. 13:10 RSV). To be insolent is to be proud and haughty. Notice again how it brings in strife. It says the insolent or proud person is heedless—heedless of what? Heedless of the fact that strife will open the door to confusion and every evil work. Heedless of the fact that strife will keep you from enjoying the will of God in your life. Heedless of the fact that God teaches you how to respond and enables you by His grace to respond in love. You can choose your response. You don't have to lose your temper. You don't have to strive and quarrel.

BE LIKE JESUS

Once again, I appeal to our Pattern Man—the One who all Christians have chosen to follow. If He's your Lord, you've made an unqualified commitment to submit to Him and His ways.

> *Yet when He was insulted He offered no insult in return. When He suffered He made no threats of revenge. He simply committed His cause to the One who judges fairly* (1 Peter 2:23 Phillips).

"Oh, I can't do that!"

"Oh, yes you can!"

Jesus enables you from within, and if you rely on Him, you can do all things through Him. Regularly renew your heart and mind in the love of God. (See First Corinthians 13:4-7.)

> The Lord's bond-servant must not be quarrel-
> some, but be kind to all…patient when wronged
> (2 Timothy 2:24 NASB).

A Christian *"has no business with quarreling. Instead, be kind to everyone and patient when wronged"* (2 Tim. 2:24 Knox[2]).

The good news is that the more we choose the way of love, the more it develops in our character and becomes our established, Christ-like response. Sow into that which is spiritual, and you will reap a spiritual harvest in accordance with the good will of God. Sow to your flesh—selfishness and pride—and you will only reap a harvest of destruction and ruin. *"Do not be deceived: God cannot be mocked. A man reaps what he sows"* (Gal. 6:7 NIV).

IT MATTERS HOW WE TREAT OTHERS

I learned when I was a newlywed that our true spirituality is measured by how spiritual we are in our own home with our own family. Some Christians do not enjoy much of God's will in their lives because they haven't learned this important truth.

> You husbands must give honor to your wives. Treat
> her with understanding as you live together….If
> you don't treat her as you should, your prayers will
> not be heard (1 Peter 3:7 NLT).

Of course, if your prayers are not heard, you won't enjoy the will of God in your life! This goes for women, too.

What's the answer? Actually the answer is very simple, and the Word of God makes it very clear. Keep yourself in the love of God, or as it says in this translation, *"Live in such a way that God's love can bless you"* (Jude 21 NLT). Always remember that faith without love equals nothing, and faith only counts when it works through love. (See First Corinthians 13:2 and Galatians 5:6.) It's been said that love is the antidote to all evils. An antidote is something that relieves, prevents, or counteracts.[3] Love will keep you in God's will, remove you from the devil's will and counteract his poison, and it will always assure you that Pandora's Box stays shut.

So we can clearly see that we have been called to live by the more excellent way of love. How we treat others matters! The idea that God's will for you will come to pass unconditionally regardless of what you do or say is *false*.

Remember, we are looking for some answers to life's tough questions. Why is it that some people always seem to have their prayers answered and with others it's very hit and miss? Do you know people who regularly enjoy the will of God and other people who rarely do? Why is it that something doesn't come to pass when you can clearly see in the Bible that it's God's will for your life?

We know that God is no respecter of persons. He loves everyone equally and without partiality. In fact, Jesus prayed to the Father and asked *"that the world will know You sent Me and will understand that You love them as much as You love Me"* (John 17:23 TLB). God proves how much He loves us by exchanging Jesus for us on the cross—amazing but true!

So what's the problem? Could it be that you have a blockage that's clogging up the flow of God, the grace of God, the will of God into your life? Have you allowed some spiritual "cholesterol" to block the flow into your spiritual heart and life? The first place I would look would be in this all-important area of love. How are you treating others? Is there any strife, envy, bitterness, or resentment that needs to be removed? Are you holding unforgiveness or harboring a grudge against someone? The good news is that you can choose to release all of that and let love rule and reign in your heart.

Let's do it—right now!

WHAT WE KNOW

1. We know that the will of God does not come to pass automatically in people's lives.

2. We know that if we enter into envy and strife, we open the door to confusion and every evil work.

3. We know that how we treat others matters—a failure to love can block our prayers and the will of God for our lives.

4. We know that "love never fails," and we can choose to keep ourselves in the love of God.

Chapter 11

WHAT "THINGS" WORK TOGETHER FOR GOOD?

God is pure goodness. Who can compare to Him? All His plans for you are good, acceptable, and perfect! You can trust Him with every aspect of your life. Remember, we've established from the Word that all things that happen in life are *not* from God.

ALL THINGS?

> And we know that **all things** work together for good to those who love God, to those who are the called according to His purpose (Romans 8:28 NKJV).

According to church tradition, this means that all situations in life, all that happens and everything that comes our way, work together for good.

Stay with me now—but I see some serious flaws in that interpretation. God is good in the most absolute sense, so anything that's truly good is of God. All things "good" work together for God. Do evil spirits work together for God? How about deception, destruction, disease, abuse, alcoholism, addiction, etc.? All things from the devil do *not* work for our good! Evil spirits do not work together with God for the good of His Church! The devil's purpose is not to help advance the purpose of God in our lives!

LOOK AT THE CONTEXT

We know that in order to arrive at the right meaning from any verse in the Bible we must look at the most important issue of the context. Context is all important! You can lift a verse out of its context and make it say whatever you want it to say. To arrive at the right meaning and interpretation of any verse, we must look at the subject matter before and after that verse. Also, we must consider what we've learned throughout the entire Bible about the particular subject we're studying.

Let's go back to Romans 8:28. Notice it begins with a conjunction, *"**And** we know that...."* A conjunction is a connector between words, phrases, or sentences; it links together what's before and after it. So in order to know what Romans 8:28 is referring to, we must look at the subject matter in the verses before it. This will show us what, *"**And** we know that all things work together for good"* is connected to.

Pay close attention to the subject matter of Romans 8:26-27 (NKJV):

> *Likewise the **Spirit** also helps in our weaknesses. For we do not know what we should pray for as*

*we ought, but the **Spirit** Himself makes interces-*
sion for us with groanings which cannot be uttered.
Now He who searches the hearts knows what the
*mind of the **Spirit** is, because **He** makes interces-*
sion for the saints according to the will of God.

The subject of these two verses is clearly the Holy Spirit. He's ready to help believers with everything in life. The word *helps* in verse 26 means that He takes hold together with us or cooperates with us and enables us to effectively intercede according to the will of God. To "cooperate" means to co-work, to act together, or to co-operate. Notice how F.F. Bruce picks this up in his translation:

We know, too, that the Spirit cooperates in every
way for good with those who love God, those whom
God has called in accordance with His eternal
purpose (Romans 8:28, Bruce[1]).

Romans 8:28 from the New English Bible makes this clear as well, *"And in everything, as we know, He cooperates for good with those who love God and are called according to His purpose." "He"* is referring to the Holy Spirit. So when the Bible refers to *"all things"* working together for good, it's referring to all the workings of the Holy Spirit who is always at work to bring about the good will of God in the earth.

What things? Here it says He enables us to intercede according to the will of God when we don't know what we should pray for. He helps and enables us with all the wonderful gifts of the Spirit. God's Word is an indispensable weapon, and it is called *"the sword of the Spirit"* (Eph. 6:17). The Holy

Spirit helps us fulfill the good will of God so we are "*clothed with power from on high*" (Luke 24:49 NASB).

In all these things and more, the Holy Spirit is working together with us for good! Don't pull verse 28 away from verses 26 and 27. It does not say that all things that happen in life work together for your good—all things in life are *not* from God! God is *not* sending things that steal, kill, destroy, deceive, or devastate. Does the context show us that the Holy Spirit works together with God to bring good into our lives, or do the devil and his works cooperate and partner with God? Romans 8:28 (alternate translation in CEV footnote) makes it clear, "*God's Spirit always works for the good of everyone who loves God.*"

PRAISE GOD FOR OR IN?

Back around 1975 I got into some books that deceived me on this issue. The author had written a series of books about the power and importance of praise. I believe his heart was right, but his teaching was drastically wrong. He operated on the false premise that since Romans 8:28 says that all things that come into our lives are allowed by God, there is always a good reason for everything that happens to us. He taught that everything that happens to you ultimately is the will of God, so you should be thankful, rejoice, and praise God for it. Remember, "extreme sovereignty" teaches that nothing happens unless God wills it to happen. (See Chapter 2.)

A true story was given in one of these books about a young father who backed out of his garage and accidently ran over his toddler son, killing him. The author actually counseled this grieving father to praise God and give thanks for the accident because all things work together for good! Confusing? Yes, to say the least!

The Bible does tell us, *"In every thing give thanks: for this is the will of God in Christ Jesus concerning you"* (1 Thess. 5:18). However, we are to give thanks *in*, not *for!* In every circumstance worship God and keep your grip of faith on Him; but give thanks for everything *God* does, not for what *satan* does!

Here are two Bible examples that clearly illustrate that we are to praise God in everything and not for everything. The first is from the Old Covenant and is found in Second Chronicles 20. Jehoshaphat is the king of Israel at this time, and word is brought to him that three enemy armies have united together to obliterate Israel. Has this been sent or allowed by God to somehow work for Israel's ultimate good? No! Notice how Jehoshaphat responded—instead of praising God *for* an enemy whose intentions were to pillage, plunder, and destroy his nation, Jehoshaphat humbled and submitted himself to God:

> *O our God...we have no power against this great multitude that is coming against us; nor do we know what to do, but our eyes are upon You* (2 Chronicles 20:12 NKJV).

God spoke to them through a prophet, assuring them the victory; and they responded by praising God *in* the midst of their circumstances.

Notice carefully that they did not praise God *for* these things that were coming against them. They showed no indication that they believed that God had determined, decreed, or willed this to happen. In fact, they didn't believe that God was behind it at all!

The king appointed singers to go out ahead of the Israeli army, and with expectant faith, they believed that God would turn this situation around for their good. As soon as they began to sing and praise the Lord, God set Himself against the three enemy armies; and in a state of confusion, they utterly destroyed one another. God worked together for the good of His people who loved Him and were called according to His purpose!

Our second example is from the New Covenant and is found in Acts 16. Paul and Silas are on their second missionary journey, and they cast a demon spirit out of a fortune teller. The girl's masters see that their hope of profit is gone, so they haul Paul and Silas before the authorities. They are judged unjustly, stripped naked, beaten with rods, their backs laid open by a Roman whip, and thrown into a dark, damp dungeon with their feet secured in stocks.

In the midst of those terrible circumstances, Paul practices his own preaching and does what the Holy Spirit tells us all to do: *"Give thanks in all circumstances, for this is God's will for you in Christ Jesus"* (1 Thess. 5:18 NIV). *"Rejoice in the Lord always. Again I will say, rejoice!"* (Phil. 4:4 NKJV). So at midnight Paul and Silas prayed and sang praises unto God, and God supernaturally delivered them out of the Roman prison! Paul and Silas took hold together with the Holy Spirit, and He cooperated with them and worked this situation out for their good.

You remember after the birth of baby Jesus, King Herod sent out a decree and had all the male babies slaughtered. He was trying to kill the Lord Jesus. (See Matthew 2.) That act was not from God, and it did not work together for the good of the parents who lost their baby sons.

I remember a friend of mine telling me about a funeral he attended. A non-Christian couple had gotten stoned on drugs and went out driving on the highway. They had a horrible head-on collision that killed them instantly. At their funeral, the minister quoted Romans 8:28, *"And we know that all things work together for good."* If this couple went out into a Christless eternity, how did that work together for their good?

I've heard some Christians say, "Well, Father God allows bad things to happen in order to teach and deepen us spiritually." Enemy soldiers don't come to teach and perfect you. They come to steal, kill, rape, pillage, and shoot flaming missiles into your house! Would you send your child to an al-Qaeda training camp in order to teach them a lesson and deepen them spiritually?

I know I'm going against the commonly held view of Romans 8:28. Church traditions are good when they're biblically sound and solid, but this is a stronghold that has exalted itself against the true knowledge of God. If you think that what's coming to you from satan is actually coming from God, you'll yield to it, submit to it, you won't resist it, you'll give place to it, you'll accept it, and you'll unknowingly allow satan to work his evil, grievous, unacceptable will into your life—and you will thwart what God actually wanted to do for you in that situation.

"*Submit yourselves therefore to God. Resist the devil, and he will flee from you*" (James 4:7). It doesn't say submit yourself to all things that come at you in life. Are you submitting yourself to God and resisting the devil, or submitting yourself to the devil and resisting the will of God? "Oh, I'd never do that!" Are you sure? Anything in life that Jesus came to destroy—resist it! Don't submit to what's authored by satan, thinking that sin, sickness, and all manner of evil will work together for your good.

THREE QUALIFIERS

It's amazing how most people completely jump over the three qualifiers that are mentioned in Romans 8:26-28. In order for the Holy Spirit to work in all things and in every way for your good, you must:

1. Cooperate—take hold together with Him, and He will work for your good.

2. Love God—truly make Him first in your life.

3. Answer the call to His purpose—redemption of humanity and the expansion of His Kingdom.

The Holy Spirit is the working Agent and Power who brings the will of God to pass in your life and in the world today; what He brings to pass is always good, acceptable, and perfect!

WHAT WE KNOW

1. All things do *not* work together for our good because all things are not from God.

2. All things of the Holy Spirit, all of His workings, *do* work together for our good.

3. This is in effect for those who cooperate with the Holy Spirit, love God, and are called according to His purpose.

Chapter 12

WHAT ABOUT JOB?

Many Bible scholars believe Job is the oldest written book in the Bible. Job's ordeal took place around 1845 B.C., about 155 years before the time of Moses and the establishing of the Old Covenant. Here's the crucial question we must answer today: Is Job's experience a pattern for suffering, or did it serve a particular purpose of God for all people and for all time?

I occasionally have someone say to me, "I guess I'm just having my own Job experience." Is it even possible today to have an experience like Job's?

THE ISSUE

The issue is very simple—satan comes before God and says, "Job's simply serving You for the blessings, for what he can get out of You—You are a big sugar daddy to him. Does Job fear You for nothing, God?" (Job 1:9-10, my paraphrase). Satan's challenge was this: no member of the human race will love and serve God from pure, selfless motives. People will only serve God for what they can get from Him.

God knew that this had to be proven false once and for all time. He knew that Job loved Him and served Him for who He was, not for what he could get out of Him. So the challenge began, "If Job suffers the loss of all he has, he will curse You to Your face!" Satan proudly surmised (see Job 1:11). The Lord responded by saying, *"Behold, all that he has is in your power; only do not lay a hand on his person"* (Job 1:12 NKJV). So satan went forth to steal, kill, and destroy.

JOB'S LOSSES

I'm going to give you what the Bible lists as Job's losses. Can you imagine all of this happening to you? It was all reported to him on the same day!

- 500 donkeys, 1,000 oxen, and all the servants but one—stolen and killed.

- 7,000 sheep and all the servants but one—destroyed by fire.

- 3,000 camels and all the servants but one—stolen and killed.

- A strong wind collapses his house—all ten children inside die.

Job's response after all of this was to worship God and maintain his faith in Him (see Job 1:20). Satan's response was to basically say to God, "Yeah, big deal! If the man's flesh and bones are affected, he will surely curse You to Your face!" (see Job 2:5). The Lord responded by saying, "*Behold, he is in your hand, but spare his life*" (Job 2:6 NKJV). So satan strikes Job with painful boils from the top of his head to the soles of his feet. His condition was so severe that when three of his friends came to visit, they didn't even recognize him.

> *My flesh is clothed with worms and a crust of dirt;*
> *my skin hardens and runs* (Job 7:5 NASB).

> *My breath is offensive to my wife, and I am loathsome to my own brothers* (Job 19:17 NASB).

His wife, who should have been his closest supporter, said to him, "*Do you still hold fast your integrity? Curse God and die!*" (Job 2:9 NASB).

That's what the devil was trying to get him to do! So to make matters worse, Job's wife is now cooperating with satan. In spite of all of this, Job remains steadfast in his faith and patient endurance. Job was 70 years old when all of this took place. Although his challenging ordeal only lasted nine months, it was so miserable it must have seemed like nine years to him!

I have faithfully been in church since I was six years old, and it amazes me how so many people, preachers included, get the details of Job and his life's story so wrong. I wonder if they've ever carefully read it. People speak so authoritatively about Job and yet leave out huge chunks of his story.

For instance, Job is commended for hanging in there—he did not reject God—but he was far from the epitome of perfection! Very few preachers tell you what Job said from chapters 3 through 31. Job quickly moves into complaining, self-justification, and self-righteousness.

Job's three friends should be there to encourage and support him; instead, they falsely accuse and unrighteously judge him. For 28 chapters, they engage in a series of arguments with Job, bantering and bickering back and forth. If you read the Book of Job in one sitting, you might have to take short time-out breaks to get away from all their arguing and strife!

Keep this in mind: Job lived before Moses and the establishing of the Old Covenant. He apparently had a limited understanding of God and very little knowledge of satan. Not one time does he mention satan as his oppressor; instead, he justifies himself and blames God. Before the end of his ordeal he had to repent of things he falsely and mistakenly accused God of. Job was like a lot of people today—he blames God for everything that goes wrong.

"I AM FULL OF CONFUSION"

"If I be wicked, woe unto me; and if I be righteous, yet will I not lift up my head. I am full of confusion; therefore see thou mine affliction" (Job 10:15). Job clearly states his problem when he admits, *"I am full of confusion."*

I am going to give you just a small sample of some of the many things that Job wrongly said about his God, to help you see that he's indeed confused and his theology is incorrect. Pay careful attention to the mistaken and confused theology of Job.

"Does it seem good to You that You should oppress, that You should despise the work of Your hands, and smile on the counsel

of the wicked?" (Job 10:3 NKJV). The truth is that God does not despise Job, God is for him and not against him, and God is not his oppressor. Jesus went about doing good and healing all that were *"oppressed"* by the devil (Acts 10:38). We do have an oppressor to contend with, but God is not our oppressor!

"Why do You hide Your face, and regard me as Your enemy?" (Job 13:24 NKJV). Job wrongly thinks that God is his enemy. Jesus identifies the enemy as the devil in Matthew 13:39. God is for Job and wants him to get through this situation in victory.

In the next few statements Job makes some harsh accusations against God.

"He tears me in His wrath, and hates me; He gnashes at me with His teeth; my adversary sharpens His gaze on me" (Job 16:9 NKJV). God does not hate Job, and God is not his adversary! You can clearly see that Job thought God was his problem—he thought he was being attacked by God.

> *I was at ease, but He has shattered me; He also has taken me by my neck, and shaken me to pieces; He has set me up for His target, His archers surround me. He pierces my heart and does not pity; He pours out my gall on the ground. He breaks me with wound upon wound; He runs at me like a warrior* (Job 16:12-14 NKJV).

So many people have had the same misunderstanding about God that Job had. Have you ever believed that God was behind all the wrong that was happening to you? We do have an enemy who hates us and seeks to tear us apart, but it's not God! God loves us with an everlasting love (see Jer. 31:3), and the steadfast love of the Lord toward us never ceases (see Lam. 3:22).

The Bible tells us that our adversary is the devil, not God:

> *Be careful! Watch out for attacks from the devil, your great enemy. He prowls around like a roaring lion, looking for some victim to devour. Take a firm stand against him, and be strong in your faith* (1 Peter 5:8-9 NLT).

Job thought that God had made him His target and was shooting His arrows at him. God is not the evil one who sets us up as His target!

> *In addition to all, taking up the shield of faith with which you will be able to extinguish all the flaming arrows of the evil one* (Ephesians 6:16 NASB).

You can clearly see that God counsels us to keep our shield of faith up at all times so that not even one arrow of the devil is able to strike us.

Listen to Job's next statement—this helps us really see what's at the root of his confused mindset.

> *If the scourge kills suddenly, He mocks the despair of the innocent. The earth is given into the hand of the wicked; He covers the faces of its judges. If it is not He, then who is it?* (Job 9:23-24 NASB).

God does not laugh and become amused at the suffering caused by plagues. He does not cover the faces of the judges so that they judge unrighteously. You can see that Job thinks God is the Author and Originator of every bad thing that happens on earth! His last statement gives us the key to his problem, *"If it is not He, then who is it?"* You see, Job had no revelation of satan, his real oppressor—the one who wanted to see him curse God and die!

WHEN GOD SHOWS UP

When God finally intervenes and speaks into this situation, He asks Job a challenging question, *"To justify yourself, will you condemn Me?"* (Job 40:8 Moffatt[1]). In Job chapters 29–32, Job uses the personal pronouns *I, me, my,* and *myself* 163 times in defending and justifying himself. That must be a Bible record! He's justifying himself instead of God.

God corrects Job by asking this question, *"Who is this that darkens counsel by words without knowledge?"* (Job 38:2 NASB). Well, it was Job! You see, his heart was right; his theology was wrong. Job had said, *"Though He slay me, yet will I trust in Him"* (Job 13:15). God wasn't Job's enemy, and He didn't want to slay him! Job had mistakenly said, "He gives and He takes away—shall we receive good at the hand of God and shall we not receive evil?" (see Job 1:21). God doesn't want to take away your children and your possessions. He didn't save you and make you His child in order to bring evil into your life!

Even with his misguided thinking and faulty theology, Job did not reject and forsake God. God clearly says that Job's words darken sound counsel, his words are not accurate and are without knowledge; and yet, amazingly, a majority of

Christians hold onto the mistaken theology of which Job had to repent!

Notice carefully what Job said after God enlightened him and corrected his wrong theology:

> *Therefore I have uttered what I did not under-stand, things too wonderful for me, which **I did not know**.... Therefore I abhor myself, and repent in dust and ashes"* (Job 42:3,6 NKJV).

For what did he need to repent? His wrong theology, which painted a grossly inaccurate picture of God's nature and God's will for people!

DO NOT BE DECEIVED

> *Don't be deceived my dear brothers. Every good and perfect gift is from above, coming down from the Father of heavenly lights, who does not change like shifting shadows* (James 1:16-17 NIV).

I find it amazing that in the very areas where the Bible warns us, "Do not be deceived," most Christians *are* actually deceived! The Lord is good, and only good gifts come from Him. He is not the author of anything bad. He is the same every day and forever. He is not a schizophrenic at the mercy of serious mood swings.

We teach our children that God is a good God, and the devil is a bad devil. God is not your enemy. He is your Helper, your Answer, your forever Friend and Savior. You are to hate what is evil and get righteously mad at all the destructive and unjust works of the devil.

Job gave no place to the devil in his theology, but you must realize that you have a personal enemy who hates you and is constantly trying to trick you into all manner of evil and tragedy. Always remember that satan hates you and has a horrible plan for your life!

> *A final word: Be strong with the Lord's mighty power. Put on all of God's armor so that you will be able to stand firm against all strategies and tricks of the devil* (Ephesians 6:10-11 NLT).

THE RESTORATION OF JOB

Let's not forget about Job's three friends. They appear on the scene to comfort Job, and, at first, they make some true statements about God and life in general. But they quickly move into their own opinions, reasonings, and unrighteous judgments, concluding that Job must be in gross sin for this to happen to him. They falsely accuse him of being a hypocrite, of sowing bad seed and now reaping a bad harvest, and of not helping the poor and needy. In doing so, they speak wrongly of Job and of God, too. (Learn this from the mistakes of Job's friends—you're better off saying nothing when you don't know for sure!)

> *And the Lord restored Job's losses when he prayed for his friends. Indeed the Lord gave Job twice as much as he had before* (Job 42:10 NKJV).

Well, what about Job? God healed him, restored two-fold all that he had lost, brought him together with his wife, and gave him seven more sons and three more daughters. Job lived another 140 years and died old and full of days at the age of 210.

Was Job's experience a pattern for all believers to come, or was it a one-time example to prove a particular point? Job never turned from God or cursed Him. So satan was proven wrong—people will love and serve God of their own free will from pure, selfless motives. They will love God for who He is, not just for what He gives.

In Job, God's purpose was met for all people, for all devils, for all time, and for all generations to come. People cannot have a Job experience today! After Job's ordeal had ended, he told his testimony for the next 140 years of his life with correct theology.

Why won't the church do that today?

IMPORTANT CONSIDERATIONS

Think this statement through—God's promises prevent reoccurrences. That sounds complicated, but it's really not. Let's look at the Great Flood as an example. After the Fall of Adam, things had deteriorated to such a condition that only Noah and his family of seven were just and walking with God.

> Then the Lord saw that the wickedness of man was great in the earth, and that every intent of the thoughts of his heart was only evil continually (Genesis 6:5 NKJV).

This is an astonishing fact! Have you ever known one person of whom you could truly say that *"every intent of the thoughts of his heart was only evil continually?"*

So we have an almost apocalyptic situation on planet Earth; with the exception of Noah and his family, the entire human race has become totally and irretrievably corrupt. Rain covered the entire earth, and Noah and his family were the only ones preserved because of the covenant promise God made with them (see Gen. 6:18).

Would God, even though He is sovereign, ever break one of His covenant promises? Never!

> *"Thus I establish My covenant with you: Never again shall all flesh be cut off by the waters of the flood; never again shall there be a flood to destroy the earth." And God said: "This **is** the sign of the covenant which I make between Me and you, and every living creature that **is** with you, for perpetual generations: I set My rainbow in the cloud, and it shall be for the sign of the covenant between Me and the earth"* (Genesis 9:11-13 NKJV).

Can the experience of Noah ever be repeated? Can we have a Noah experience today? No! Why not? God established a covenant promise that forever settled the issue. The promise cancels out the reoccurrence.

Remember that Job lived 155 years before the time of Moses and the Old Covenant. Job could not look to the promises of the Old Covenant given to Moses and his generation simply because they had not yet been given! Notice what Moses could confidently say regarding himself and anyone else who would make the Lord their refuge and fortress by trusting Him and dwelling in His sheltered place of covenant promise:

He who dwells in the secret place of the Most High shall remain stable and fixed under the shadow of the Almighty [Whose power no foe can withstand]. I will say of the Lord, He is my Refuge and my Fortress, my God; on Him I lean and rely, and in Him I [confidently] trust!...

You shall not be afraid of the terror of the night, nor of the arrow (the evil plots and slanders of the wicked) that flies by day, nor of the pestilence that stalks in darkness, nor of the destruction and sudden death that surprise and lay waste at noonday.

...Because you have made the Lord your refuge, and the Most High your dwelling place, there shall no evil befall you, nor any plague or calamity come near your tent. For He will give His angels [especial] charge over you to accompany and defend and preserve you in all your ways [of obedience and service]... (Psalm 91:1-11 AMP).

Just as you may have made Psalm 23 yours and found great comfort in it, you can equally do the same with Psalm 91. Notice how David puts his trust in the same covenant promise:

For in the day of trouble He will hide me in His shelter; in the secret place of His tent will He hide me; He will set me high upon a rock. And now shall my head be lifted up above my enemies round about me... (Psalm 27:5-6 AMP).

Isaiah clearly stated and put his trust in the promise of the covenant as well:

> *But no weapon that is formed against you shall prosper, and every tongue that shall rise against you in judgment you shall show to be in the wrong. This [peace, righteousness, security, triumph over opposition] is the heritage of the servants of the Lord...* (Isaiah 54:17 AMP).

A heritage is simply that which you have inherited by way of the covenant that God has made with you. As born-again believers who are living under the New Covenant, we now have a better covenant, better promises, a better High Priest, and better everything than there has ever been in any previous age.

> *But now He has obtained a more excellent ministry, inasmuch as He is also Mediator of a better covenant, which was established on better promises* (Hebrews 8:6 NKJV).

It has been said that God in His sovereignty can override any of His promises whenever He chooses to because He is God. That's utterly false and ridiculous! That would make God out to be a covenant-breaker, a liar, and would destroy the confidence of His children. God is not a human being who makes promises that He does not intend to keep; it is impossible for Him to lie.

WHAT WE KNOW

1. The challenge of Job has been met—for all people and for all time.

2. All the promises God has made since Job's time
   assure us that a "Job experience" is not possible
   for believers living under the New Covenant.

Chapter 13

WHAT ABOUT SUFFERING?

I have often been asked this question, "Aren't Christians sup-posed to suffer?" I answer that question by saying, "Yes, absolutely!" But you must keep one very important factor in mind—God never intends for you to suffer what Jesus came to alleviate, eradicate, and destroy! We'll come back to this very important distinction later in this chapter.

CHRIST—OUR EXAMPLE

Christ is our example in suffering, just as He is in all other areas of life, and we are to follow His example.

> *This suffering is all part of what God has called you to. Christ, who suffered for you, is your example. Follow in His steps* (1 Peter 2:21 NLT).

What did Jesus suffer in His walk here on earth? Let's take a look at the list.

- Jesus was tempted by satan (see Matthew 4, Hebrews 2:18).

- Falsely accused of blasphemy (see Matthew 26:65).

- Falsely accused of being a sinner (see John 9:24).

- Falsely accused of being a criminal (see John 18:30).

- Falsely accused of being a glutton and a drunk (see Matthew 11:19).

- Falsely accused of being a devil (see John 8:48).

- Falsely accused of being out of His mind (see Mark 3:21).

- They also said, "This man is not from God" (see John 9:16 NKJV).

- Jesus suffered persecution (see John 5:16).

- He was laughed at and mocked (see Matthew 9:24).

- He suffered rejection (see Matthew 8:34).

- He was betrayed (see Matthew 26:48).

- He suffered perils in the city (see John 8:59).

- He suffered perils among false brethren (see Luke 22:2).

- He was spit upon (see Matthew 26:67).

- Arrested (see Matthew 26:57).

- Jailed (see Matthew 27:1).

- Beaten (see Matthew 26:67).

- And flogged with a lead-tipped whip (see Mark 15:15).

The Bible makes it clear and actually promises that we will suffer persecution also. Jesus said:

> *When the world hates you, remember it hated Me before it hated you. The world would love you if you belonged to it, but you don't. I chose you to come out of the world, and so it hates you. Do you remember what I told you? "A servant is not greater than the master." Since they persecuted Me, naturally they will persecute you. And if they had listened to Me, they would listen to you! The people of the world will hate you because you belong to Me, for they don't know God who sent Me. This has fulfilled what the Scriptures said: They hated Me without cause"* (John 15:18-21,25 NLT).

Jesus promises that His followers:

> *Will get more than they left. Here in this world they will have a hundred times more homes, brothers, sisters, mothers, children, and fields. And with those things, they will also suffer for their belief...* (Mark 10:30 NCV).

So we can be assured that if we truly follow Jesus, we will certainly suffer persecution. *"In fact, everyone who wants to live a godly life in Christ Jesus will be persecuted"* (2 Tim. 3:12 NIV).

THE EARLY CHURCH SUFFERED

Notice how this was confirmed in the lives of the original disciples. What they suffered was a mirror image of what Jesus suffered! Let's take a look at the list:

- They suffered temptation (see 1 Corinthians 10:13).

- They were falsely accused of blasphemy (see Acts 6:13).

- They were falsely accused of wrongdoing (see Acts 25:7-8).

- They were slandered and reviled for their good behavior in Christ (see 1 Peter 3:16).

- They suffered persecution (see Acts 8:1).

- They suffered rejection (see Acts 21:36).

- They suffered shame (see Acts 5:41).

- They were mobbed (see Acts 21:30-32).

- They were stoned (see Acts 7:58).

- They were beaten (see 1 Corinthians 4:1).

- They were severely flogged (see Acts 16:23).

- They were arrested (see Acts 16:23).

- They were chained like criminals (see 2 Timothy 2:9).

- Many were martyred (see Acts 7:60).

Included in the list of their sufferings are: reviling, slanders, false accusations, rejections, evil reports, despising, misunderstandings, defamation, disapproval, shame for His name, discrimination, tortures, hatred from the world, and hatred from their own relatives. Whenever they suffered according to the will of God, they counted it all joy, rejoicing that they were counted worthy to suffer shame for His name! They kept in their hearts and minds what Jesus had taught them:

> *Blessed are those who are persecuted for righteousness' sake, for theirs is the kingdom of heaven. Blessed are you when they revile and persecute you, and say all kinds of evil against you falsely for My sake. Rejoice and be exceedingly glad, for great is your reward in heaven, for so they persecuted the prophets who were before you* (Matthew 5:10-12 NKJV).

SUFFERINGS THAT ARE NOT ACCORDING TO THE WILL OF GOD

You have just read a list of sufferings that are according to the will of God. Absent from this list are things like depression, disease, demon possession, mental torment, guilt, condemnation, broken-heartedness, etc. I repeat, God never intends for you to suffer what Jesus came to alleviate, eradicate, and destroy.

> *...The Son of God appeared for this purpose, to destroy the works of the devil* (1 John 3:8 NASB).

> *You know of Jesus of Nazareth, how God anointed Him with the Holy Spirit and with power, and how He went about doing good and healing all who were oppressed by the devil, for God was with Him* (Acts 10:38 NASB).

> *And thus He fulfilled what was spoken by the prophet Isaiah, He Himself took [in order to carry away] our weaknesses and infirmities and bore away our diseases* (Matthew 8:17 AMP).

Some people mistakenly think that a disease, a mental problem, a broken heart is their "cross to bear" or their "thorn in the flesh." God would never make you bear what Jesus came and bore away upon Himself—that would be a gross injustice—to you and to Jesus! No, those kinds of things are sufferings that are not according to the will of God.

The Bible shows us that there are two distinct categories of suffering. One is the category of suffering that we partake of with Christ as His followers. We always know that this is suffering according to the will of God. Persecutions, insults, distress, and opposition for the gospel's sake is what is being referred to in the following Scriptures:

> *And if we are [His] children, then we are [His] heirs also: heirs of God and fellow heirs with*

Christ [sharing His inheritance with Him]; only we must share His suffering if we are to share His glory (Romans 8:17 AMP).

For to you it has been granted for Christ's sake, not only to believe in Him, but also to suffer for His sake (Philippians 1:29 NASB).

For just as the sufferings of Christ are ours in abundance, so also our comfort is abundant through Christ (2 Corinthians 1:5 NASB).

The other category of suffering is never according to the will of God. Sin, sickness, bondage, and all manner of evil are clearly shown to be works of the devil. We don't have to be oppressed by that whole category of suffering since Jesus came as our Liberator, Healer, and Savior!

WHAT ABOUT PAUL'S THORN?

I'm really perplexed as to why so many Christians have had such a difficult time arriving at the correct answer concerning Paul's thorn. Perhaps they've never clearly and carefully read this portion of Scripture. The vast majority of people think Paul had some type of incurable disease that God gave to him! Let's read Paul's own testimony and believe what he tells us:

And lest I should be exalted above measure by the abundance of the revelations, a thorn in the flesh was given to me, a messenger of Satan to buffet me, lest I be exalted above measure. Concerning

> *this thing I pleaded with the Lord three times that it might depart from me. And He said to me, "My grace is sufficient for you, for My strength is made perfect in weakness." Therefore most gladly I will rather boast in my infirmities, that the power of Christ may rest upon me. Therefore I take pleasure in infirmities, in reproaches, in needs, in persecutions, in distresses, for Christ's sake. For when I am weak, then I am strong* (2 Corinthians 12:7-10 NKJV).

Paul plainly tells us that this *thorn* was a messenger of satan. The Greek word for messenger, *angelos,* is used 188 times in the Bible. It is translated "angel" 181 times and "messenger" the other 7 times. In all 188 instances, it refers to a person, never to a thing. An angel or a messenger is always a person and never a sickness or disease.

This messenger Paul refers to is a satanic personality. There is no personality to a disease. In referring to this messenger of satan, Rotherham's translation uses the personal pronoun "he."[1] Weymouth's translation says, *"As to this, three times I besought the Lord to rid me of **him.**"*

When Paul tells us so clearly what this "thorn" was, why would we say it was something else? Why would people refuse to take Paul at his own word and twist the Scriptures? Paul had been told by Jesus right after his conversion *"how many things he must suffer for My name's sake"* (Acts 9:16 NKJV). This is exactly what the Lord Jesus said to Ananias. Paul enumerates a large list of sufferings that were instigated by this *"messenger of Satan."* All of Paul's letters were written without chapter and verse divisions, so notice how the context of chapter 11 flows together with chapter 12:

> ...*In far more labors, in far more imprisonments, beaten times without number, often in danger of death. Five times I received from the Jews thirty-nine lashes. Three times I was beaten with rods, once I was stoned, three times I was shipwrecked, a night and a day I have spent in the deep. If I have to boast, I will boast of what pertains to my weakness* (2 Corinthians 11:23-25,30 NASB).

Paul not only tells us that his thorn was a satanic angel, he also tells us what that angel came to do. He said that he was sent *"to buffet me,"* in the same way that waves buffet a boat or the soldiers buffeted Christ. Notice Weymouth translates it this way, "*Satan's angel dealing blow after blow*" (2 Cor. 12:7 Weymouth). Paul suffered in his body a steady stream of persecution as this *"messenger of Satan"* regularly stirred up evil men to deal him *"blow after blow."*

Just from the whippings alone, he received 195 lashes! No wonder he could say:

> ...*For I bear on my body the [brand] marks of the Lord Jesus [the wounds, scars, and other outward evidence of persecutions—these testify to His ownership of me]!* (Galatians 6:17 AMP).

God did not promise to take away the buffetings that often come with persecutions; in fact, He promised that until He returns, we will always have persecution and tribulation. He did promise us that His grace would be sufficient, enabling us to bear and endure any and all types of persecution for Christ and His gospel's sake.

Here's how Apostle Paul settled the issue:

> But He said to me, "My grace is sufficient for you, for My power is made perfect in weakness." Therefore I will boast all the more gladly about my weaknesses, so that Christ's power may rest on me. That is why for Christ's sake, I delight in weaknesses, in insults, in hardships, in persecutions, in difficulties. For when I am weak, then I am strong (2 Corinthians 12:9-10 NIV).

Clearly absent here is any kind of sickness or disease; they would be under the category of sufferings that are not according to the will of God.

> Many evils confront the [consistently] righteous, but the Lord delivers him out of them all (Psalm 34:19 AMP).

Apostle Paul could gladly say:

> You know how much persecution and suffering I have endured. You know all about how I was persecuted in Antioch, Iconium, and Lystra—but the Lord rescued me from all of it (2 Timothy 3:11 NLT).

Paul could confidently say, "For just as the sufferings of Christ are ours in abundance, so also our comfort is abundant through Christ" (2 Cor. 1:5 NASB).

What Jesus said to the Apostle Paul He says to all of us as well, "My grace is sufficient for you!"

WHAT WE KNOW

- All who live godly in Christ Jesus suffer persecution (see 2 Timothy 3:12).

- Persecution is not strange or unusual for Christians (see 1 Peter 4:12).

- It is an honor, not a shame, to suffer as a Christian (see 1 Peter 4:16).

- Suffering persecution glorifies God (see 1 Peter 4:14).

- His grace will be sufficient for you. His Spirit will rest upon you (see 2 Corinthians 12:9 and 1 Peter 4:14).

- There will be a great reward in Heaven for you, so rejoice whenever you are persecuted! (see Matthew 5:12).

- There is a category of suffering that is according to His will (see 1 Peter 4:19).

- There is a category of suffering that is not according to His will (see 1 John 3:8; Acts 10:38, Luke 13:16).

Chapter 14

THE FEAR FACTOR?

Most of us have heard the old idiom, "The two go together like oil and water." In other words, the two just don't mix! When it comes to faith and fear, this is most definitely true. When fear comes in, faith goes out.

The Bible is full of cases in which God reveals His will to His people, telling them clearly what He wants them to have, and they allow fear to enter in and thwart the will of God for their lives! We must remember that it's always by faith and patience that we enter into the promises of God—we are to "*imitate those who through faith and patience inherit the promises*" (Heb. 6:12 NKJV).

Fear is one of the biggest roadblocks to the will of God coming to pass in your life. I am sure that an entire book could be written on this factor of fear. Fear works like a negative kind of faith—it focuses on failure, misfortune, calamity, ruin, and all manner of negativity. Notice how this truth is confirmed in the following Scripture:

> *All the days of the desponding and afflicted are made evil [by anxious thoughts and forebodings],*

but he who has a glad heart has a continual feast [regardless of circumstances] (Proverbs 15:15 AMP).

Notice this verse clearly says that if you dwell in anxious thoughts and forebodings, all your days are made evil! Here's the definition of foreboding: "to have an inward conviction of coming ill or misfortune, a presentiment of coming evil."[1] You are actually expecting evil and misfortune to come! This helps bring to pass the very things you've been dreading.

As I've said previously, what you believe rules you. You're drinking a deadly cocktail mixed with anxiety and fear. When your negative expectation finally comes to pass, you cry out, "I was afraid that was going to happen!"

I want to tell you another story that's sad but true. I grew up in Kansas in a neighborhood that was full of boys, all close to my age. We played sports together year-round—baseball, football, basketball, and track. All of us had a lot of athletic ability, and when we entered junior high together, our sports teams were outstanding.

One of our teammates was about 6 feet tall, weighing 180 pounds at the age of 14. But he had a mother who was overprotective and seemed to worry incessantly about him. "Dear, did you take your vitamins? Don't go outside without your sweater! Did you drink your four glasses of water this morning? Don't forget to wear your gloves!" She gave him a steady stream of this day and night. When he turned 16, she allowed him to go to a summer sports camp. On the way home from that camp, he was tragically killed in an accident. As hard as it may be, I must ask the question, "To what degree did all those years of fear factor into this situation?"

THE BELIEVER'S ENVIRONMENT

For anything to live and thrive, it must dwell in its proper environment. If you want a thing to stagnate, become paralyzed, and finally die, simply remove it from its environment. Fish need the sea, birds need the air, plants need the soil—everything grows in its own environment. Strip something of its environment, and you eliminate its power to survive.

The Christian's environment is the Truth. If you abide in Jesus (Truth) and His Word (Truth) abides in you, you will bear much fruit (see John 15:7-8). In other words, you will live and thrive, enjoying the promises and will of God in your life!

The word abide is *meno* in the Greek language. It can also be translated, "dwell, remain, or continue in."[2] The Truth is your dwelling place. It's the environment of the believer. Jesus assures us:

> *If you abide in My word, you are My disciples indeed. And you shall know the truth, and the truth shall make you free* (John 8:31-32 NKJV).

It's clearly the will of God for all Christians to enjoy the God-kind of freedom. Not only does His Truth make you free, but that Truth keeps you free. But you must continue to dwell, abide, and stay in your proper environment—His Truth! *"I have no greater joy than to hear that my children walk in truth*" (3 John 4 NKJV). Can you clearly see that's the realm for which we were made?

THE DEVIL'S ENVIRONMENT

Just as germs and bacteria thrive in an environment of filth, the devil has an environment he thrives in as well. His environment is the realm of the lie. The devil's environment is everything that is based on and rooted in a lie—everything that departs from the environment of the Truth. Everything that is false is the environment of the devil.

Jesus actually confirms and reveals this truth to us:

> *The devil...does not stand in the truth, because there is no truth in him. When he speaks a falsehood, he speaks what is natural to him, for he is a liar [himself] and the father of lies and of all that is false* (John 8:44 AMP).

That is his craft and trade—his specialty—and he is the master of deception. He is the expert when it comes to lies and falsehood—after all, he invented them.

Now watch carefully how this works. Whenever you reject the Truth in any area of your life, as a consequence, you believe the lie. In any given situation, you believe either the Truth or the lie. When you reject the Truth, you've effectively given the devil permission to deceive you in that particular area or issue in your life. When you believe a lie, you've entered the wrong environment!

Since what you believe rules you in every area of your life, I ask this question, "What do you currently believe?" In any given area of your life, you're either in Truth and faith or in the lie and unbelief. Unbelief is not non-belief; it's not a position where you believe nothing. You always believe something about everything. Unbelief is wrong belief—it's believing the lie.

Are there areas of your life where you are currently paralyzed by believing the lie—unbelief? The devil knows he can keep you out of the will of God in any given area of your life if he can get you to buy the lie. If I buy the lie, then that's what rules in that particular area of my life. *The devil can only touch you where you believe a lie—that's his environment!*

STAY IN YOUR ENVIRONMENT

A former teacher of mine taught me this truth years ago, *"Abide* in the Truth, and you're devil-proof!" Remember, Jesus said in John 8:44 that the devil cannot abide or stand in the Truth. In fact, the Truth expels him and uproots his lie; and not only does the Truth *make* you free, it *keeps* you free (see John 8:32). Take away the devil's environment—the realm of the lie—and he's powerless! Strip something of its environment, and you eliminate its power to survive. Satan cannot operate in the environment of the Truth.

Jesus, as always, is our Example—our Pattern Man. When satan presented his lies to Him in the wilderness, Jesus stayed in His native environment—the Truth—and He responded with the Truth, *"It is written!"* (Matt. 4:4-10). Jesus lived His whole life in the environment of the Truth, and that's why He could always say that the devil *"has no claim on Me. [He has nothing in common with Me; there is nothing in Me that belongs to him, and he has no power over Me]"* (John 14:30 AMP).

YOU MUST DEAL WITH THE LIE!

It's been said, "Fear is always built on a lie—deal with the lie, and fear will die!" You deal with the lie by replacing it with God's Truth—what has God said about this situation? God's Word brings faith with it; when faith comes in, fear goes out! Fear cannot abide or dwell in the environment of the Truth. You eliminate fear's environment by dwelling in the environment of the Truth. Faith is always built on the Truth—live in the Truth, and you're fear-proof.

Take note of this, when God says to you, "Fear not"; He's telling you that you are going to be in situations that will try to move you into fear. But you don't have to fear, because God assures you over and over, "I am with you!"

> *…Fear not, for I have redeemed you; I have called you by your name; you are Mine. When you pass through the waters, I will be with you; and through the rivers, they shall not overflow you. When you walk through the fire, you shall not be burned, nor shall the flame scorch you* (Isaiah 43:1-2 NKJV).

Notice that God says as you're going through these things, He will be with you, so fear not! If you falsely believe that the problem or challenge is bigger than God's ability to bring you through, you're buying the lie and opening the door to fear. Fear will only bring failure and keep you out of God's good will for your life.

King David learned this lesson well, *"Yea, though I walk through the valley of the shadow of death, I will fear no evil; for You are with me"* (Ps. 23:4 NKJV). David knew he would get through it because God was with him! That's why he could boldly say, *"I will fear **no** evil!"*

As a believer, you can also boldly say, "I will not fear!" God is with us—He is perfect love—and perfect love casts out *all* fear (see 1 John 4:18). It's been said that there are 365 "fear nots" in the Bible—one for every day of the year.

OLD TESTAMENT PROOF

Remember when the 12 spies were sent out to see what Canaan was like? This was God's Promised Land for the entire nation of Israel. Without question, entering into this promise was God's will for every one of them. *"Send men to spy out the land of Canaan, which I am giving to the people of Israel"* (Num. 13:2 ESV). The 12 spies come back and report that the land is a wonderful place with an abundance of marvelous fruit and produce. But there is also an abundance of giant enemies that will have to be faced and dispossessed.

God had already given them His Word and made it very clear that it was His will for every one of them to have Canaan, "the Promised Land," as their possession. The 12 spies came back, and 10 of them acted like God hadn't spoken, wasn't with them, and had lied to them! What was their problem? They had entered into the Thomas Syndrome. (See Chapter 8.) "We will only believe in what we can *see*—if something doesn't *look* like the will of God, then it must not be the will of God."

The physical realm was primary and final authority to them—it's where their belief was based.

> *...we saw the descendants of Anak there....all the people whom we saw in it are men of great stature. There we saw the giants...and we were like grasshoppers in our own sight, and so we were in their sight* (Numbers 13:28,32-33 NKJV).

As they rejected the Truth, they entered into unbelief and the wrong environment. Remember, fear is always built on a lie, and the lie is the environment of the devil. Watch now how the lie produces fear in the entire nation: "*So all the congregation lifted up their voices and cried, and the people wept that night*" (Num. 14:1 NKJV).

No wonder God calls this an "*evil report*" (Num. 13:32); it was faithless—rooted in fear and unbelief. These people were defeated by a lie before they ever attempted to step out in faith with God. You see, it's true that what you believe rules you. Although it was God's will for the entire nation to go in, only Joshua, Caleb, and all those under 20 years of age possessed the promise.

Fear will effectively block the will of God and keep it from coming to pass in your life! This is just one of many Bible proofs that the will of God is not automatic.

Now notice what the other two spies, Joshua and Caleb, believed and said about the same situation: "*The Lord is with us: fear them not*" (Num. 14:9). In other words, "Abide in the Truth with us—there's no fear here—the Lord is with us!"

Caleb had already said, *"Let us go up at once and possess it; for we are well able to overcome it"* (Num. 13:30).

Were they *"well able"* to possess it? Why? God had given them His Word that this land was His will for them. God says He is always *"alert and active, watching over My word to perform it"* (Jer. 1:12 AMP). Caleb knew that the Lord would work with them and confirm His Word (see Mark 16:20).

These two spies realized that their environment was the Truth. Their faith was based on God and His Word; it was anchored to the unseen and spiritual realm. They knew that believing would lead to seeing the promise of God fulfilled. So with their faith in the unseen realm of God and His Word, they could confidently say, "Fear not—the Lord is with us—let's go up and possess it, for we are well able!" God is pleased when we believe Him (see Heb. 11:6), so He commended His servant Caleb for having a "different spirit" than the ten unbelieving spies (see Num. 14:24).

> *And since we have the same spirit of faith, according to what is written, "I believed and therefore I spoke," we also believe and therefore speak* (2 Corinthians 4:13 NKJV).

Caleb chose to stay in that "spirit of faith," and you and I can, too! We do not have to be plagued and tormented by fear, allowing it to block the will of God for our lives. In Caleb and Joshua we have clear examples of how, through faith and patience, we inherit the promises and enter into the will of God (see Heb. 6:12).

NEW TESTAMENT PROOF

We see the same thing played out in the life of Apostle Peter. Now remember, God would not have to remind us continually to "fear not" if we never encountered situations that tried to draw us into fear. So here's the next situation: After a full day of ministry, Jesus sends His disciples off, while He spends time in prayer on the mountainside. The disciples are hit by a tremendous storm as they are attempting to cross the sea. At around 3 A.M., Jesus comes out to them, walking on the sea.

Since this is the first time in history that anyone had ever walked on water, they naturally think that they are seeing a ghost! *"But immediately Jesus spoke to them, saying, 'Be of good cheer! It is I; do not be afraid'"* (Matt. 14:27 NKJV). Here's another "Fear not!" Jesus doesn't want them to get in the wrong "environment." Are you starting to see the importance of environments?

Peter basically said, "Lord, if that's really You, call me to come to You on the water." So Jesus gave him His Word and His will: "Come on!" Then Peter got out of the boat and walked on the water toward Jesus. We now have the second man in history to ever walk on water. But suddenly Peter had a faith failure. He moved from the believer's environment over into the devil's environment.

Jesus wanted to help Peter, and He wants to help us as well, so He asks the question, *"Why did you doubt?"* (Matt. 14:31 NKJV). Let's take a closer look and learn from Peter's mistake.

When Peter steps out, his faith is based on Jesus and His Word. He's staying in the right environment; as long as his eyes are on Jesus, he's experiencing the supernatural will of God! But when he shifted his focus from Jesus over to the things of the natural realm, he left his proper environment. Just like the ten spies, he forgot what Jesus said, and he made the physical realm his final authority: *"But when Peter saw the wind and the waves, he became afraid and began to sink"* (Matt. 14:30 NCV).

So Jesus asks this all-important question, not just to Peter, but to all of us, *"Why did you doubt?"* The Greek word *distazo* that Jesus uses here for doubt means "to stand in two ways," implying uncertainty over which way to take.[3] In other words, "Should I look to Jesus (spiritual realm) or to these things that say, 'Impossible, forget it, you're not going to make it' (natural realm)?" Remember, faith and fear are like oil and water—the two just don't mix.

When fear comes in, faith goes out. We can clearly see with Peter that when he takes his eyes off Jesus, fear leaps in, and doubt is always connected with fear.

It was the Lord's will that Peter walk with Him on the water; it was not God's will that he sink! He had a faith failure when Jesus was personally with him. Peter did not lose faith in Jesus or Father God over this particular incident, but you can see in this water-walking situation, that when fear came in, faith went out, and that answers Jesus' question, *"Why did you doubt?"*

Have you ever found yourself in a predicament like Peter's? Before you stepped out you made sure you had the Word of the Lord and you knew you were moving in the will of God; and the next thing you know, the strong winds of circumstance change, and you begin to fail.

Maybe you're in that kind of situation right now? Do a quick inventory! Have you stayed in the believer's environment of Truth? Have you lost your focus on Jesus and His Word? Have you taken account and given consideration to the fear factor?

If you feel like you're sinking, I want to encourage you! Peter made a quick adjustment and jumped right back into his proper environment. He put his full faith-focus back on Jesus, and immediately he was lifted up!

FEAR NOT—BELIEVE ONLY

Here's a great example of someone who stayed in his proper environment. He was determined to abide in the Truth—Jesus and His Word—even when his situation went from bad to worse. Let's look at the true story of Jairus, a ruler of one of the synagogues.

Jairus had a 12-year-old daughter who was sick and at the point of death. When he came to Jesus, he said to Him, *"Come and lay Your hands on her, that she may be healed; and she shall live"* (Mark 5:23). Notice there was no hesitancy or uncertainty in Jairus' request. He didn't say, "I know You are sovereign and if it be Your will, she shall live." There was no doubt in Jairus' mind about the matter. He knew that Christ was the Healer, and that healing was His will, so Jairus said, *"She shall live"* (Mark 5:23).

Could it be that Jairus had heard the Good News that Jesus *"went about doing good and healing all"* and how *"He went about all the cities and villages healing every sickness and every disease among the people"*? (Acts 10:38, Matt. 9:35).

Could Jairus have heard and believed the words of Jesus when He said, *"He who has seen Me has seen the Father"* (John 14:9 NKJV) and when Jesus said that He came *"to do the will of Him who sent Me"* (John 4:34 NKJV)? How else could Jairus have known that when Jesus got to his daughter, she would be healed and she would live? His faith was solidly rooted in the Truth that Christ was the healer and healing was God's will for his daughter.

Before they could reach the house, a messenger came and said to Jairus, "Your daughter has died; don't trouble the Master about this anymore." If that wouldn't take all of the faith out of your sails, what would? If you had been Jairus, how would you have responded? Jesus immediately gives Jairus His word, *"Fear not: believe only, and she shall be made whole"* (Luke 8:50).

Jesus tells him the Truth, and Jairus is immediately faced with a choice—he can abide in the Truth and see the will of God take place, or he can hook up with fear and see God's will short-circuited. Why would Jesus tell Jairus, *"Fear not: believe only"* if we have no choice or part to play in the matter?

If "extreme sovereignty" and omnicontrol are how God chooses to work, why wouldn't Jesus have said something like, "If God sovereignly chooses to heal your daughter, Jairus, she shall be healed regardless of fear and doubt." Why tell him to resist fear and believe, as if he had any part to play in the matter?

Because our part is to abide in the Truth—believe and stay out of fear. God's part is to do the supernatural. Jesus spoke His all-powerful word to Jairus' daughter, and she was up immediately, breathing again, and ready for something to eat! (See Luke 8:55.)

WHAT WE KNOW

1. The believer's environment is the Truth.

2. The devil's environment is the lie.

3. Fear will keep you out of God's will for your life.

4. Always replace fear with the Truth—what has God said about the situation?

Chapter 15

THE ULTIMATE ANSWER

...And let us run with endurance the race that God has set before us. We do this by keeping our eyes on Jesus, on whom our faith depends from start to finish... (Hebrews 12:1-2 NLT).

Life is a journey, a long distance race that must be run and navigated with our focus riveted on Jesus from start to finish. Jesus perfectly shows us the heart, character, and will of God the Father. If you form your understanding of God and His will from any other source but Christ, you will end up with a wrong conclusion—a misunderstanding. Our understanding of God, His will, ourselves, and the true condition of this present world cannot be formed by our experience, our reason, or even our interpretation of the Bible apart from Christ. We need a solid rock we can anchor ourselves to, and that Rock is Christ alone!

"GO TELL JOHN"

There are times in our lives when we are hit with situations that make our heads spin and leave us wondering, "What happened?" Nothing about our situation seems to fit what we know about God, so we ask the question, "Why?"

Let's look closely at how John the Baptist found himself in this exact dilemma. Remember, John the Baptist had been chosen by God to prepare the way for the coming Messiah. Jesus said of John that there was not a greater prophet born of women (see Luke 7:28).

When John saw Jesus coming to his baptism, John said, *"This is He....I have seen and testified that this is the Son of God"* (John 1:30,34 NKJV). When John baptized Jesus, he saw the Holy Spirit descend on Him like a dove, and he heard the Father's voice from heaven say, *"This is My beloved Son, in whom I am well pleased"* (Matt. 3:16-17). No one could have received a clearer revelation from God that Jesus was Savior and Messiah. John the Baptist was sure of this—no doubt about it!

But notice what we humans have a tendency to do when the winds of adversity blow against us. After John had fulfilled his ministry, he was taken captive and placed in Herod's prison. He then sent two of his disciples to Jesus to ask Him, *"Art thou He that should come? or look we for another?"* (Luke 7:19). How did John move from a place of certainty, *"This is He,"* to a place of uncertainty and doubt, *"Art thou He"*?

When you focus on what could have happened or what didn't happen instead of what's already happened—all that God has done and revealed to you—you create a fertile seedbed for doubt, skepticism, and unbelief. Notice, in essence, that what Jesus tells the disciples to go tell John is this—Go tell John the testimonies!

> *And that very hour He cured many of infirmities, afflictions, and evil spirits; and to many blind He gave sight. Jesus answered and said to them, "Go and tell John the things you have seen and heard: that the blind see, the lame walk, the lepers are cleansed, the deaf hear, the dead are raised, the poor have the gospel preached to them"* (Luke 7:21-22, NKJV).

Go tell John the testimonies! Every testimony recorded in the Bible forever establishes and clearly portrays who Jesus is and what the will of God is for all people on planet Earth.

Here's a lesson we must learn along with John the Baptist—don't let the questions you can't answer destroy the foundation of the truths you already know!

> *The secret things belong unto the Lord our God: but those things which are revealed belong unto us and to our children forever...* (Deuteronomy 29:29).

The things that Jesus and the Word reveal to us belong to us so that we can know and embrace the will of God. It is, therefore, always of utmost importance to know what is and what is not from God. Jesus' life, actions, and teaching clearly show us that there are wills other than God's will that have no other purpose than to wreak havoc and bring evil upon humanity. Jesus spent His life waging war upon these evil entities and bringing healing, deliverance, forgiveness, and relief in order to set the captive human race free!

We don't compromise and forsake what we do know when we are confronted by situations that hit us with a big *Why?* Remember, we live in a fallen world that is besieged by forces that hate God and all that is good. With confidence, we keep ourselves anchored in Jesus and our eyes fixed on Him, the Author and the Finisher of our faith (see Heb. 12:2).

In the midst of a volatile world where we don't always understand what happened or why, we *do* understand that God the Father looks just like Jesus. In every situation in life we know that the Father's heart, will, and purpose for us are exactly the same as those of Jesus. We know that all the nightmarish occurrences of life are never from God.

Jesus and the Bible reveal that they come from satan, evil spirits, and people who knowingly or unknowingly cooperate with them. We know that evil events are called "evil" for that exact reason—they originate from the evil one. Even though we live in a cosmic war zone with evil agents always strategizing against us, we know that God and His agents are always with us to support us.

Jesus tells us:

> I have told you these things, so that in Me you may
> have [perfect] peace and confidence. In the world
> you have tribulation and trials and distress and
> frustration; but be of good cheer [take courage; be
> confident, certain, undaunted]! For I have over-
> come the world. [I have deprived it of power to

> *harm you and have conquered it for you]* (John
> 16:33 AMP).

The Bible assures us again, *"If God be for us, who can be against us?"* (Rom. 8:31).

JESUS ERASES THE SCARS

It is only fitting at this point that I share with you a true story, a testimony, of a friend of mine. She was born into a home in which both parents were addicted to drugs and alcohol. Her childhood was filled with a barrage of beatings—boards, bats, and even barbed wire were used against her. She was stabbed twice, shot once, and suffered many broken bones. By the time she entered her 20s, her body was covered with scars and was severely weakened and damaged.

She was moved from foster home to foster home, over 20 in all, and continued to be severely disciplined if she dropped a plate or broke a glass, etc. Her victimized life could clearly be characterized as one that was void of love. What had happened to her? Why? Who was behind such acts of terror? Was there a way out for her? How? Could she find love, peace, healing? She needed a new life, a new start, a new beginning. Was this even possible? Did God care? Was He there?

At the age of 27, for the first time, my friend heard the greatest news that the world has ever heard. She heard that Jesus, the Son of God, came into the world to take upon Himself our suffering, our abuse, our damage, our guilt and shame, so that we could have new life from Heaven and a brand-new start. She heard that Jesus came to give her life, not more of the same life she'd had, but His kind of life, the life that you see in Him.

She gladly received His gracious gift and took Him as her Lord and Savior. She experienced the miracle of the second birth, and a new spiritual life was imparted into her. The Bible tells us that if any person will come into Christ they will be made a new creature; the old spiritual and moral conditions will pass away and everything will become fresh and new (see 2 Cor. 5:17).

My friend experienced the greatest of all miracles, that glorious new birth, but what about her physical condition? Did her newly found Savior, Jesus Christ, have any desire or ability to help her physically? She wore knee braces, limped with both feet, and her body was filled with crippling arthritis. When she went out in public, she kept her body completely covered so that others could not see her many scars.

Our church has regularly scheduled healing meetings, and over the years we have seen the risen Christ heal hundreds and hundreds of people. Jesus is not dead, He is alive! What He did in Bible days, He is still doing today. Wherever Jesus went, in cities, villages, and synagogues, He emphasized teaching, preaching, and physical healing. (See Matthew 4:23; 9:35.)

No one has ever been authorized to delete healing from the ministry of Jesus. When the gospel puts such an emphasis on healing, why would anyone want to change or disregard it today? We are clearly told in the Bible to pray for one another so that we may be healed (see James 5:16) and to lay our hands upon the sick so that they can recover (see Mark 16:18).

My friend came for the first time to a special healing service we were conducting. She heard the speaker confidently say that healing was God's will for people and that Jesus was there to heal people right then. She said, "I sat listening, almost afraid that God could or would heal me. I was so afraid that He would say no to my healing." When people were asked to come forward for prayer, she sat there frozen until a friend came over and ushered her to the front.

One of the healing team members from the church, a woman, asked her what she needed prayer for. She asked for the most impossible thing she could imagine—new skin without scars. The woman prayed a very direct and surprisingly short prayer and then asked if there was anything else. My friend gave her the entire list—crippling arthritis in her feet, knees, hips, elbows, wrists, and hands. The woman prayed over each body part specifically and had her move each part as she prayed. To the astonishment of my friend, her flexibility came back almost immediately, and she was pain-free in minutes!

In the time that it took her bones and joints to be healed, her skin had begun to itch to the point of making her miserable. She excused herself and went to the restroom. She took wet paper towels and began to dampen her skin, hoping that would bring relief. To her amazement, she realized that the skin she had been wiping was now smooth. Those rough and ridged scars on her arms and stomach had completely disappeared! Her arms were smooth, her stomach was smooth, her legs were smooth, and even the scars on her feet were gone!

She had worn knee braces for more than six years and had not been able to support herself without them. She said, "I felt like I had to do knee bends, which was completely nuts because I couldn't do knee bends at all—period. So I took off my pants and my braces there in the church restroom. I tried one and went all the way down and all the way up. Then I cried—not from pain, but from happiness!"

My friend left the meeting that night free from the arthritic pain that had plagued her for years, scar-free with fresh new skin, and carrying her knee braces. Evil spirit beings and people who had yielded to them had victimized her, but Jesus came to destroy those devilish works and erase all the damage that had been done. She met Christ, the Healer, that night, and to Him goes all the praise and all the glory forever!

This woman became a member of our church and was with us for about five years. She recently moved to the country, where she now owns and tends her own livestock. Her story will live on forever as it tells, first of all, what happened—how all the evil, unfair occurrences in her life had subjected her to spiritual and physical bondage. Her story more importantly testifies of the One who redeems from all bondage; it proves that Christ is the Ultimate Answer and that He is still the same today!

GET BACK TO JESUS

Do you know the difficulty in our day is that we have run away from Jesus? That is, the church at large has. The world is making a great struggle at the present hour, and we are in the midst of it ourselves, to get back to Jesus. We have run into false theology, we have run into "churchanity" and human interpretations, and a hundred other follies, but friends, it is a perfectly lovely and refreshing thing to get back to Jesus. Take the words of Jesus and let them become the Supreme Court of the Gospel to you.

If our questions were settled by the words of Jesus, we would be out of all the confusion that the world is in at present. I do not see any other way for the world to come out of her present confusion unless it is to accept the words of Jesus as final authority, to accept Jesus as the divine finality where all questions are finally adjudicated, and stay by the words of Jesus. —John G. Lake[1]

JOURNEY'S END

So our journey to find the answer to life's every difficult "Why?" ends with the Ultimate Answer—Jesus. He's coming soon to eradicate everything that's inconsistent with His loving will and purpose for us—no more sin, sickness, depression, abuse, heartache, injustice—no more death!

Jesus is going to come again to destroy all foes once and for all; He will then establish a forever kingdom where perfect love, peace, harmony, and justice will reign forever.

...I go to prepare a place for you. And if I go and prepare a place for you, I will come again and

receive you to Myself; that where I am, there you may be also (John 14:2-3 NKJV).

And so our place will be with Him—forever! *Maranatha!* Come, O Lord!

WHAT ABOUT ISRAEL AND JACOB, AND PHARAOH'S HARDENED HEART?

ISRAEL AND JACOB

The subject matter of Romans 9 and 11 has been used to confuse, confound, and disillusion more people than possibly any other portion of Scripture in the entire Bible. To arrive at its proper meaning, we must remember to pay close attention to its subject matter and take into account what is taught about the subject throughout the whole Bible. Let's consider these Scriptures together:

> ...When Rebecca also had conceived by one man, even by our father Isaac (for the children not yet being born, nor having done any good or evil, that the purpose of God according to election might stand, not of works but of Him who calls), it was said to her, "The older shall serve the younger." As it is written, "Jacob I have loved, but Esau I have hated" (Romans 9:10-13 NKJV).

> *For the Scripture says to the Pharaoh, "For this very purpose I have raised you up, that I may show My power in you, and that My name may be declared in all the earth." Therefore He has mercy on whom He wills, and whom He wills He hardens* (Romans 9:17-18 NKJV).

Upon a surface reading, this could sound like God randomly chooses some people to be saved and other damned—He has mercy on some and hardens others—He loves some and hates others simply by His random choice, before they were ever born. A large number of people actually teach and believe that! But is this the subject of these Scriptures, and is this what God is teaching us here?

THE ANSWER IS IN THE DETAILS

It's of the utmost importance that we pay attention to the details and stick with the subject matter of any portion of Scripture. God summarizes this particular teaching through Apostle Paul by saying this about the nation of Israel:

> *Concerning the gospel they are enemies for your sake, but concerning **the election** they are beloved for the sake of the fathers. For **the gifts** and **the calling** of God are irrevocable* (Romans 11:28-29 NKJV).

Notice these terms—*"the election," "the gifts,"* and *"the calling of God,"* are all in reference to the nation of Israel. The word election simply means picked out or chosen. We know that the nation of Israel did not work for and earn their place as "the chosen of God." They are simply "the elect" of God—His sovereign choice. Paul lists some of their "gifting"—God revealed His glory to them, made covenants with them, gave His law to them, the temple service and the promises (see Rom. 9:4). All of this was according to His sovereign choice—His "election."

Paul is not addressing individual salvation in Romans 9, as so many mistakenly conclude—in fact, he does not refer to that subject one time in this context. He emphasizes the way that God picked out Israel, giving them a chosen assignment to serve Him and the world; so the subject here is election to service, not the salvation of every individual who will ever live!

The apostle emphasizes this issue again with the example of Jacob and Esau:

> *For the children not yet being born, nor having done any good or evil, that the purpose of God **according to election** might stand, not of works but of Him who **calls** (Romans 9:11 NKJV).*

God "called" Jacob over Esau, clearly showing His choice of Jacob's descendants (the nation of Israel) over Esau's descendants (the Edomites). Once again, this verse is not referring to individual salvation, but rather the priestly purpose that God chose for the nation of Israel. If you try to interpret Romans 9 as the way that God saves or damns individuals, you are ignoring the subject matter and fabricating what it simply does not say.

Election has to do with *gifts* and *callings*, not individual choice and responsibility.

LOVE-HATE?

What does it mean when it says, *"Jacob I have loved but Esau I have hated?"* (Rom. 9:13 NKJV)? This was an idiom used in those days to express preference, not personal malice or hatred. Notice in what context the Lord Jesus used it:

> *If anyone comes to Me and does not hate his father and mother, wife and children, brothers and sisters, yes, and his own life also, he cannot be My disciple* (Luke 14:26 NKJV).

Jesus is not teaching us that we should hate all others, including ourselves, and only love Him. He is teaching us to "prefer" and put Him first above all others, even above ourselves. So "Jacob I have loved" refers to *choice* and *calling*, meaning that God "preferred" to work through Jacob rather than Esau. Jacob was God's "preference," His sovereign choice.

THE CALL OF GOD

This is not a strange concept or teaching; in fact, we find it all the way through the Bible.

> *To be a high priest is an honor, but no one chooses himself for this work. He must be called by God as Aaron was. So also Christ did not choose Himself to have the honor of being a high priest, but God chose Him* (Hebrews 5:4-5 NCV).

People have always been "chosen" for ministry according to the "election" of God, not of works but of Him who "calls."

(See Romans 9:11.) Any individual cannot "choose" to be a pastor, for instance, like they would choose to be a police officer, fire fighter, or accountant—that's not an individual's prerogative! It's all according to the "election" or choice of the sovereign God who "calls."

Here are a few more examples of the way God calls.

Jeremiah the Prophet—"*Then the word of the Lord came to me saying: 'Before I formed you in the womb I knew you; before you were born I sanctified you; I ordained you a prophet to the nations'*" (Jeremiah 1:4-5 NKJV).

John the Baptist, Prophet—"*He will also be filled with the Holy Spirit, even from his mother's womb. And he will turn many of the children of Israel to the Lord their God. He will also go before Him in the spirit and power of Elijah…to make ready a people prepared for the Lord*" (Luke 1:15-17 NKJV).

Paul the Apostle—"*But when it pleased God, who separated me from my mother's womb and called me through His grace*" (Galatians 1:15 NKJV).

In every one of these cases, the call of God for service and ministry was made according to the election and choice of God. He called these individuals by His grace before they were ever born; so, obviously, it was not according to their works. To confirm this once again, the subject in Romans 9 is God's election and call to ministry and service, not individual salvation.

WHAT ABOUT THE HARDENING OF PHARAOH'S HEART?

Let's take a quick refresher about Pharaoh and the Israelites. God's chosen people, Israel, had been under severe bondage to the nation of Egypt for 430 years. God elected and sent forth a prophet named Moses to be His representative and mouthpiece before Pharaoh, the ruler of Egypt. Before God sends Moses to face Pharaoh, He basically reveals this to Moses, "I am going to instigate a series of miraculous signs for Pharaoh. The end result of all My dealings with Pharaoh will be this—they will simply serve to harden his heart even more against Me and My chosen people; but after all My dealings with Egypt, Pharaoh will surely let you go!" (See Exodus 3:20; 4:21.)

The miraculous signs and plagues begin. After the second plague, Scripture tells us this: *"But when Pharaoh saw that there was relief,* **he hardened his heart** *and did not heed them, as the Lord had said"* (Exod. 8:15 NKJV). After the fourth plague, we see that he chooses to resist the dealings of God again. *"But* **Pharaoh hardened his heart** *at this time also; neither would he let the people go"* (Exod. 8:32 NKJV). After the seventh plague, we see that Pharaoh still resists the dealings of God and refuses to repent, *"And when Pharaoh saw that the rain, the hail, and the thunder had ceased,* **he** **sinned yet more; and he hardened his heart,** *he and his servants"* (Exod. 9:34 NKJV).

Now notice what the very next verse says, *"So the heart of Pharaoh was hard; neither would he let the children of Israel go"* (Exod. 9:35 NKJV). God had given this man seven chances to reconsider, humble himself, soften, and repent; but after all these dealings of God, Pharaoh chose to continue in his sin and harden his heart against God even more.

LEARN THE WAYS OF GOD

Now before the eighth plague, the Lord said to Moses, *"Go in to Pharaoh; **for I have hardened his heart** and the hearts of his servants"* (Exod. 10:1 NKJV). Here are some important lessons to learn about the ways and workings of God.

Early church father Origen (185-254) taught this:

> Since we consider God to be both good and just, let's see how the good and just God could harden the heart of Pharaoh. Perhaps by an illustration used by the apostle in the Epistle to the Hebrews, we can show that, by the same operation, God can show mercy to one man while he hardens another, although not intending to harden. "The ground," he says, "drinks in the rain that falls upon it and produces crops for the farmer, being blessed by God. But the ground that produces thorns and briars is worthless, and is in danger of being cursed. Its end is to be burned." (see Hebrews 6:7-8)
>
> It may seem strange for Him who produces rain to say, "I produced both the fruit and the thorns from the earth." Yet although strange it is true. If the rain had not fallen, there would have been neither fruit nor thorns. The blessing of the rain, therefore, fell even on the unproductive land. But since it was neglected and uncultivated, it produced thorns and thistles. In the same way,

the wonderful acts of God are like the rain. The differing results are like the cultivated and the neglected land."[1]

Finis Dake's commentary says:

God hardens on the same ground as showing mercy. If men will accept mercy, He will give it to them. If they will not, thus hardening themselves, He is only just and righteous in judging them. Men are privileged to humble themselves and seek mercy or exalt themselves and refuse mercy. Mercy is the effect of a right attitude, and hardening is the effect of stubbornness or the wrong attitude toward God. It is like the clay and the wax in the sun. The same sunshine hardens one and softens the other. The responsibility is with the materials, not with the sun. Men are more responsible than these materials, for they have wills to make proper choices. The only sense in which God hardened Pharaoh was in giving him the occasion to harden his own heart or obey. Such is the choice all men make daily.[2]

That is why Scripture says, "*God opposes the proud but gives grace to the humble*" (*James 4:6 NIV*). And, "*For everyone who exalts himself will be humbled, and he who humbles himself will be exalted*" (Luke 14:11 NIV).

We see this all the way through the entire Bible. God does not "make" the proud *proud*, nor does He "make" the humble *humble*. People can choose to humble themselves before God or exalt themselves before God. They can choose to submit and soften themselves or rebel and harden themselves. It's been said that choice settles destiny, and that's very true! Your own choice will determine your outcome. Notice how this proved to be true in the life of Israel's first king.

King Saul started out with a humble heart, but his heart grew proud and rebellious:

> *Samuel said, When you were small in your own sight, were you not made the head of the tribes of Israel, and the Lord anointed you king over Israel?* (1 Samuel 15:17 AMP)

King Saul chose to reject the authority of God, and he became increasingly rebellious and hardened in his heart against God. King Saul's continual decisions to reject the ways and the words of the Lord eventually settled his outcome:

> *For rebellion is as the sin of witchcraft, and stubbornness is as iniquity and idolatry. Because you have rejected the word of the Lord, He also has rejected you from being king* (1 Samuel 15:23 NKJV).

Individuals settle their own destinies by choosing to put their faith and trust in God or choosing to rebel and reject Him: *"If we deny and disown and reject Him, He will also deny and disown and reject us"* (2 Tim. 2:12 AMP).

Notice how this principle of God being like the sun that has a hardening effect on some materials and a softening effect on others is clearly seen in Romans, chapter 1. Here we have a description of the type of people who stubbornly and persistently choose to rebel against God and His ways. We are told that

> ...since they did not see fit to acknowledge God or approve of Him or consider Him worth the knowing, God gave them over to a base and condemned mind to do things not proper or decent but loathsome (Romans 1:28 AMP).

This phrase, "God gave them over," is also used in verses 24 and 26. In other words, God won't violate a person's free will and make them do what they don't want to do. But the end result is that their foolish hearts are darkened (see Rom. 1:21). As they continue to reject God and harden their hearts against Him, their lives are flooded with all manner of vile filth and depravity. They experience in themselves the truth of this saying, "No greater punishment can any man have than to be left to have his own way."

> You might call us in our work for God the means whereby the fragrance of Christ comes to those who are on the way to salvation and to those who are on the road to ruin. For those who are on the way to ruin it is a deadly and poisonous stench; for those who are on their way to salvation it is a living and life-giving perfume (2 Corinthians 2:15-16 Barclay[3]).

So we can see that the same gospel has a hardening effect on some and a softening effect on others. It hardens those who resist it and reject it; and it softens those who humble themselves and receive it.

WHAT WE KNOW

1. Election, as referred to in Romans chapters 9 and 11, has to do with God's call to ministry and service, not the salvation of every individual who has ever lived.

2. Every individual is responsible for how he or she chooses to respond to the gospel. Those who humble themselves and receive are softened; those who rebel and reject are hardened.

ENDNOTES

CHAPTER 1

1. Koran, Surat Al-Hadid 57:22.

2. Koran, Surat As-Saffatt 37:96.

3. Augustine, *Enchiridion,* Library of Christian Classics, ed. J. Baille, J. McNeill, and H.P. Van Duren, trans. A.C. Outler (Philadelphia: Westminster Press, 1955), 395.

4. Augustine, *City of God* 5.10; *Nicene and Post-Nicene Fathers, First Series,* ed. Alexander Roberts, James Donaldson, Philip Schaff, and Henry Wace, 14 vols. (Peabody, MA: Hendrickson Publishers, 1994), 2:93.

5. John Calvin, *Institutes of the Christian Religion,* ed. James T. McNeill, trans. Ford L. Battles (Philadelphia: Westminster Press, 1960), 198-199 [1.16.2].

6. Latif Yahia and Karl Wendl, *I Was Saddam's Son* (New York: Arcade Publishing, 1997).

7. Ibid., 152-154.

8. Ibid., 45.

CHAPTER 2

1. *Webster's American Family Dictionary* (New York: Random House, Inc., 1998).

CHAPTER 3

1. Scripture quotations marked CEV are from Contemporary English Version, copyright © 1995 by the American Bible Society, New York, NY. All rights reserved.

2. *The American Heritage Dictionary of the English Language,* Fourth Edition (Boston, MA: Houghton Mifflin Co., 2007).

3. Augustine, *Enchiridion,* 395.

4. Augustine, *City of God* 5.10; *Nicene and Post-Nicene Fathers, First Series,* 2:93.

5. John Calvin, *Institutes of the Christian Religion,* 198-199 [1.16.2].

6. Justin Martyr, *2 Apology* 5; *The Ante-Nicene Fathers,* ed. A. Roberts and J. Donaldson, 10 vols. (Grand Rapids, MI: Eerdmans, 1979), 1:190.

7. Ibid.

8. Clement of Alexandria, *Stromata* 1.17; Roberts and Donaldson, 2:319.

9. Tertullian, *Apology* 22; Roberts and Donaldson, 3:36.

10. Tertullian, *Exhortation on Chastity* 2; Roberts and Donaldson, 4:50-51.

11. Origen, *Against Celsus* 4.65; Roberts and Donaldson, 4:527.

12. John Calvin and John T. McNeill (ed.), Institutes of the
    Christian religion, Volume 1, Book ,(Westminster John Knox
    Press, Louisville, KY, 2008), p. 200

13. Origen, *Against Celsus.*

CHAPTER 4

1. *Webster's American Family Dictionary* (New York: Random
    House, Inc., 1998).

2. Augustine, *Enchiridion,* 395.

3. John Calvin, *Institutes of the Christian Religion,* 198-199
    [1.16.2].

4. Charles Spurgeon, "God's Will About the Future," sermon
    (No. 2242), delivered at the Metropolitan Tabernacle,
    Newington, England, October 16, 1890; on-line archive:
    The Spurgeon Archive—Spurgeon's Sermons; http://www.
    spurgeon.org/sermons/2242.htm; accessed June 22, 2011.

5. Koran, Surat Al-Hadid 57:22; Surat As-Saffatt 37:96.

6. Charles Spurgeon, "Free Will—A Slave," sermon (No. 52),
    delivered at New Park Street Chapel, Southwark, England,
    December 2, 1855; http://www.spurgeon.org/sermons/0052.
    htm; accessed June 21, 2011.

7. Charles Spurgeon, "A Jealous God," sermon (No. 502),
    delivered at the Metropolitan Tabernacle, Newington,
    England, March 29, 1863; http://www.spurgeon.org/
    sermons/0502.htm; accessed June 21, 2011.

8. *Webster's Encyclopedic Unabridged Dictionary of the English
    Language* (Beaverton, OR: Dilithium Press, Ltd., 1989).

9. Origen, *First Principles* 3.5.8; *The Ante-Nicene Fathers,* ed. A. Roberts and J. Donaldson, 10 vols. (Grand Rapids, MI: Eerdmans, 1979), 4:344.

10. Irenaeus, *Against Heresies* 5.37; Roberts and Donaldson, 1:518.

11. Athenagoras, *A Plea for the Christians* 24; Roberts and Donaldson, 2:142.

12. Scripture quotations marked Williams are from Williams New Testament by Charles B. Williams, The New Testament in the Language of the People (Chicago: Moody Press, 1966).

CHAPTER 5

1. Scripture quotations marked Wuest are from Wuest New Testament, Kenneth S. Wuest, The New Testament, An Expanded Translation (Grand Rapids, MI: William B. Eerdmans Publishing Co., 1961).

2. H.D. McDonald, *The God Who Responds* (Minneapolis, MN: Bethany House Publishers, 1986), 26.

3. *Epistle to Diognetus* 7.4 (2nd century AD, early example of Christian apologetics), *The Apostolic Fathers: Greek Texts and English Translations of Their Writings,* ed. and trans. by J.B. Lightfoot and J.R. Harmer, ed. and rev. by M.W. Holmes (Grand Rapids, MI: Baker, 1992), 545.

4. C.S. Lewis, *Mere Christianity* (1943); on-line pdf file: http://www.truthaccording toscripture.com/documents/ apologetics/mere-christianity/Mere-Christianity.pdf, 26; accessed June 22, 2011.

5. Justin Martyr, *1 Apology* 43; *The Ante-Nicene Fathers,* ed.
   A. Roberts and J. Donaldson, 10 vols. (Grand Rapids, MI:
   Eerdmans, 1985). Justin's defenses to the Romans are the
   oldest Christian apologies still in existence.

6. Clement of Alexandria, *Miscellanies* 1.17; Roberts and
   Donaldson, 1985.

7. Christian Martyr Methodius, *The Banquet of the Ten Virgins,*
   8.16; Roberts and Donaldson, 1985.

8. Archelaus, *Disputation with Manes* 32, 33; Roberts and
   Donaldson, 1985.

9. Irenaeus, *Against Heresies* 5.26.2; *The Ante-Nicene Fathers,*
   ed. A. Roberts and J. Donaldson, 10 vols. (Grand Rapids, MI:
   Eerdmans, 1979), 1:555.

10. Ibid., 5.37; Roberts and Donaldson 1979, 1:518.

11. Origen, *Commentary on John* 2.7; Roberts and Donaldson,
    1979, 10:330-331.

12. Clement of Alexandria, *Stromata* 1.17; Roberts and
    Donaldson, 1979, 2:319.

13. Origen, *Against Celsus* 4.66; Roberts and Donaldson, 1979,
    4:527.

CHAPTER 6

1. *Webster's New Collegiate Dictionary* (Springfield, MA: G. & C.
   Merriam Co., 1981).

2. James Strong, *The Exhaustive Concordance of the Bible*
   (McLean, VA: MacDonald Publishing Company, n.d.).

3. Scripture quotations marked NEB are from The New English Bible (New York: Oxford University Press, 1971).

4. W.E. Vine, *Vine's Expository Dictionary of New Testament Words* (Iowa Falls, IA: Riverside Book and Bible House, n.d.).

5. Scripture quotations marked RSV are from The Holy Bible, The Oxford Annotated Bible, Revised Standard Version, copyright © 1962 by Oxford University Press, Inc., Division of Christian Education of the National Council of Churches of Christ in the USA.

6. Scripture quotations marked Phillips are from Phillips New Testament, J.B. Phillips, trans., The New Testament in Modern English (New York: The Macmillan Company, 1960).

7. Bob Dylan, "Slow Train Coming," Columbia Records, 1979.

CHAPTER 8

1. Scripture quotations marked ESV are from The Holy Bible, English Standard Version ® (ESV®), copyright © 2001 by Crossway, a publishing ministry of Good News Publishers. Used by permission. All rights reserved.

2. Scripture quotations marked NBV are from New Berkeley Version, The Modern Language Bible, The New Berkeley Version (Grand Rapids, MI: Zondervan Publishing House, 1969).

3. P.J. Madden, *The Wigglesworth Standard* (New Kensington, PA: Whitaker House, 1993), 80-81.

CHAPTER 9

1. *Webster's American Family Dictionary* (New York: Random House, Inc., 1998).

2. "WWJD?" stands for "What Would Jesus Do?"

CHAPTER 10

1. *Webster's New Collegiate Dictionary* (Springfield, MA: G. & C. Merriam Co., 1981).

2. Scripture quotations marked Knox are from Knox New Testament by Ronald A. Knox, The New Testament of Our Lord and Saviour Jesus Christ: A Translation from the Latin Vulgate in the Light of the Greek Originals (London: Burns & Oates, 1957).

3. *Webster's New Collegiate Dictionary.*

CHAPTER 11

1. Scripture quotations marked Bruce are from Bruce's Epistles of Paul, F.F. Bruce, An Expanded Paraphrase of the Epistles of Paul (Palm Springs, CA: Ronald N. Haynes Publishers, Inc., 1981).

CHAPTER 12

1. Scripture quotations marked Moffatt are from The Bible: James Moffatt Translation by James A.R. Moffatt. Copyright © 1922, 1924, 1925, 1926, 1935 by HarperCollins San

Francisco. Copyright © 1950, 1952, 1953, 1954 by James A.R. Moffatt. All rights reserved.

CHAPTER 13

1. Joseph Bryant Rotherham, *The Emphasized Bible* (Grand Rapids, MI: Kregel Publications, 1976).

CHAPTER 14

1. *Webster's New Collegiate Dictionary* (Springfield, MA: G. & C. Merriam Co., 1981).

2. W.E. Vine, *Vine's Expository Dictionary of New Testament Words,* (Iowa Falls, IA: Riverside Book and Bible House, n.d.).

3. Ibid.

CHAPTER 15

1. John G. Lake, Sermon, "Spiritual Dominion," *John G. Lake: The Complete Collection of His Life Teachings*, compiled by Roberts Liardon (Tulsa, OK: Albury Publishing, 1999), 439-440.

APPENDIX

1. Origen, *First Things,* Book 3, Chapter 1, paraphrased and abridged; David W. Bercot, *Will the Real Heretics Please Stand Up* (Henderson, TX: Scroll Publishing Co., 1989), 81.

2. Finis Jennings Dake, *Dake's Annotated Reference Bible* (Lawrenceville, GA: Dake's Bible Sales, Inc., 1961), 168, NT.

3. Scripture quotations marked Barclay are from The New Testament, A New Translation by William Barclay. Copyright © 1968 by Collins Clear-Type Press, London. All rights reserved.

ABOUT STEVE C. SHANK

Steve C. Shank is founder and senior pastor of City on the Hill Ministries International and Confirming the Word Bible College in Boulder, Colorado. He has spent most of his adult life training and equipping believers in Bible schools and churches around the world. His missions travels have taken him to the Orient, Asia, India, Africa, Russia, Europe, South America, and Central America as well as to many island nations.

He has seen Jesus heal a multitude of diseases in response to the prayer of faith. On one missions trip, he witnessed the healings of 36 blind, 36 deaf, and 12 mute people. His radio broadcast, "The God-Kind of Life," can be heard daily.

If you would like to contact Steve C. Shank or arrange for him to come to your area, church, or Bible school, please write, e-mail, or call:

Steve Shank

7483 Arapahoe Ave.

Boulder, CO 80303-1511

E-mail: pastorsteve@cityonthehill.com

Office: 303-440-3873

www.SteveCShank.com

IN THE RIGHT HANDS, THIS BOOK WILL CHANGE LIVES!

Most of the people who need this message will not be looking for this book. To change their lives, you need to put a copy of this book in their hands.

> *But others (seeds) fell into good ground, and brought forth fruit, some a hundred-fold, some sixty-fold, some thirty-fold* (Matthew 13:8).

Our ministry is constantly seeking methods to find the good ground, the people who need this anointed message to change their lives. Will you help us reach these people?

> *Remember this—a farmer who plants only a few seeds will get a small crop. But the one who plants generously will get a generous crop* (2 Corinthians 9:6).

EXTEND THIS MINISTRY BY SOWING
3 BOOKS, 5 BOOKS, 10 BOOKS, OR MORE TODAY,
AND BECOME A LIFE CHANGER!

Thank you,

[signature]

Don Nori Sr., Founder
Destiny Image
Since 1982

DESTINY IMAGE PUBLISHERS, INC.

"Promoting Inspired Lives."

VISIT OUR NEW SITE HOME AT
WWW.DESTINYIMAGE.COM

FREE SUBSCRIPTION TO DI NEWSLETTER

Receive free unpublished articles by top DI authors, exclusive
discounts, and free downloads from our best and newest books.

Visit www.destinyimage.com to subscribe.

Write to: Destiny Image
              P.O. Box 310
              Shippensburg, PA 17257-0310

Call: 1-800-722-6774

Email: orders@destinyimage.com

For a complete list of our titles or to place an order
online, visit www.destinyimage.com.